CATCH UP
INVESTING
FOR BABY BOOMERS AND GEN X'ERS MAKING UP FOR LOST TIME

Bob Carter GBA, ALMI, CIM

Dedication

This book was written for everyone who has suffered some sort of financial, physical or relationship setback and now needs to make up for lost time in their savings plans.

This book reflects some, but not all of the wisdom shared with me over the years by my life's mentors. Mike, Richard and Mark, I am forever in your debt.

This book and my life have been blessed with the love, guidance and support shared with me by my parents. Thank you for giving me everything that mattered.

My life is made better by my step-children, Reanna and Chris. Thank you for making me almost as much an integral part of your lives – as I've made you in mine. I love and am fiercely proud of you both.

My life is and always will be inspired by my wife and best friend. Thank God they are both the same person! Susan; I love you and will forever be grateful for the gifts of family you've given me and the life we've built together. The future is ours!

Table of Contents:

Forward

About You

You are between 40 – 60 years of age and not entirely confident your investments are structured well and working hard enough to ensure your financial future.

You earn good money today but that hasn't always been the case.

You haven't always contributed to your retirement and tax sheltered investment accounts and wonder if at your age, it makes sense to start?

Perhaps you are a small business owner and are just now hitting your stride?

You may have experienced divorce, illness, significant business setback or investment loss.

Up until now, your investment strategy has relied entirely on public market investments including: stocks, bonds, mutual funds and GICs.

You're not sure your financial advisor is sharing with you, all the investment options products and strategies available – and wonder why?

You stress and wonder if you can "catch up" and build the retirement income you need to secure the kind of future you deserve.

Time marches on.

About me.

I was you; less than ten years ago.

CHAPTER 1

My Story: Our Journey

In 1993, I started a career as a Financial Advisor with a major independent Canadian investment firm. I was one of the oldest "rookies" in my class at Age 33 and licensed to sell stocks, bonds and mutual funds. I was also dual-licensed to sell life insurance. Life insurance products to help my clients secure their families from catastrophe and create estate plans to transfer wealth to the next generation. Everything was going well. I had a growing practice, thoroughly enjoyed and cared about my clients and always put their interests first. I thought I could do it all.

Until I discovered, I couldn't.

In 1998, I started a small distribution business selling products to municipal and industrial fire departments, oil and gas companies, power utilities and mining operations. It was an exciting time but my partners and I failed to manage the company. We lacked the required finances and growth that the business and our shareholders deserved and the trials of working two full time jobs nearly broke me.

I lost my shirt.

I avoided declaring bankruptcy and while I was able to maintain my strong credit rating – I pretty much sacrificed everything else personally and financially to make sure everyone was paid and made as "whole" as possible. I sold the business and negotiated fair and on-going compensation for our shareholders. I supported my business partner (coincidentally, my *now* ex-wife) and a technical advisor who helped demonstrate our product.

It was the year 2000, the new millennium. It dawned on me that things would continue to get worse before they got better and that I would soon need to start the long journey back to financial health, wealth and stability.

Fast-forward to 2004. I started a new and entirely wonderful relationship with the woman I am blessed, to still call my wife and best friend, Susan. Catch Up Investing is the story of how together, we started the journey back.

Together, we spent time to rebuild our finances and stem the flow of money into our losing business venture. Things started to get better. My income stabilized and in early 2010, we made a conscious decision to take charge of our finances and start building wealth. We started by reading books, taking courses and listening to generous friends and mentors - way smarter and more successful than us. We took action and today we're doing well, Thank God.

At the beginning of 2019, it occurred to me that there might be other people in the same or similar position as we found ourselves, back in 2004. I decided to share what we learned and describe here, how we have been able to:

- Control over $1.0 Million in rental income producing real estate

- Invest in several Real Estate Construction Limited Partnerships (target and realized annualized returns on exited deals in excess of 20%)

- Invest in several Multi-tenant Limited Partnerships (target and realized annualized returns on exited deals in excess of 15%)

- Invest in several Private Equity market holdings as an Accredited Investor

- Find the silver lining in our past investment and business catastrophe.

- Take advantage of investment and business losses suffered in the past and offset future taxes using proven Canada Revenue Agency supported strategies

- Diversify our family wealth, including hard assets to protect against the erosion of our money's purchasing power and the mountains of debt our government seems unwilling to stop

- Build nearly $2.0 Million Net Worth (still growing); and

- Work towards a financial future that makes sense for us.

Today – we are both 59 years old and couldn't be more excited about the future.

Our Catch Up Investing Journey

I have one simple goal for those kind enough and curious enough to have selected and purchased this book. Together, we will explore ways you can make up for lost time and choose investments that might not be offered by conventional financial planners, stock brokers and bank sales reps, no matter where you live. I must however warn you; while there are investment options that will be highlighted in this book that carry a higher risk/reward profile compared to what you've been doing in the past – there are no get-rich-quick schemes here.

We chose to include real assets in our investment mix. We will define exactly what is an "asset". You might be surprised that you've been misled, perhaps for your entire adult life as to its true meaning. We will also explore the concept of how we responsibly used leverage or "other people's money" to create momentum and help us achieve our goals in a more compressed time frame. Finally we'll spend much, if not most of our time considering the investments that very few industry experts will show you or even discuss, because they often fail to serve them as sales people – or they are not licensed and allowed to sell them.

As I mentioned from the beginning; this project is our endeavor to give back and share our experiences with investors like you. The lessons we learned are applicable in almost every country. They apply most if you are making decent money as a single or couple today, have equity in your home or access to a reasonable amount of investment capital and are willing to step ever so slightly outside your comfort zone. Taking that step is what's necessary to achieve growth – in anything.

My wife and I live in a semi-rural community just outside Toronto, Ontario Canada. As you would expect – our investment experience resides almost entirely in this country, although we have also invested in US real estate. Some of what we will share here will be of specific interest only to Canadians. I will hi-light these sections with a Red Maple Leaf and the label them "🍁 Canadian Eh?" There will be something here for everyone as the principles translate just as easily to Americans, Australians and Britons.

We will share with you what has worked for us and what could have worked better. Everything written here will describe what options we considered and some of those we didn't but now wish we had included.

Please:

Do not expect everything in this book to work for you. Investment carries risk. I want you to be sure you speak with an accounting professional and lawyer (where needed) before you even think of committing funds. Nothing in this book constitutes personal advice as I do not know you personally nor do I know your circumstances. We will discuss the types of coaches and advisors you will need and the qualifications they should bring to the table.

We called these people our "Personal Board of Directors" and that seems like a great place for us to start.

CHAPTER 2

Your Personal Board of Directors

I don't know everything. I don't know anyone who knows everything. I DO know a number of people who know a lot more about the things that have become important to us on our Catch Up Investing journey. We've come to rely on them to help us shorten the learning curve and keep us out of trouble. Whenever we ignored their advice – we usually found ourselves on the wrong side of making a good decision. That sucks but, provided hard and valuable lessons along the way.

So what exactly is a "Personal Board of Directors"?

In 1993, I wrote a column for Profit Magazine explaining the concept. As the name suggests, it's a collection of individuals you assemble to serve in the same capacity as would a similar group of professionals whose job it is to advise a private or public company or service organization. Directors serve as mentors who have a duty to make responsible recommendations to guide progress and consider the well-being of either shareholders or the venture in general.

Unlike a corporate Board, you are not required to pay all of your directors (accountants and lawyers however, *do* expect to be paid) but you should at least invite them for lunch every once in a while and don't expect them to pick up the tab, at least not all the time.

Envisioning your future success – you owe it to yourself and your family to assemble a board of your own. But who do you include?

Well let's start with the basics.

The first role on your personal board would be that of an advisor to help you track your progress, provide tax-planning advice and help you determine whether or not you should invest and hold assets personally or through an incorporated structure. More often than not, this person will be some sort of professionally registered accountant.

While professional accreditation is important – as is good rapport – we felt it was vital to work with an advisor who was also an investor in the same kinds of vehicles as we chose. In our case, "Janet" is also a real estate investor and like us, chose to diversify away her holdings from a simple stock portfolio. She also diversified her wealth using real estate beyond the value she built up in her practice and has been a very successful role model for us. This to us, made her uniquely qualified to understand us that much better than would an accountant who never walked a mile in our shoes.

When we did our search, we learned that Janet had been a senior partner with one of the 5 largest international accounting firms but left the big shop to start her own practice where she could live a lifestyle not that much different than our own. We like working with as many like-minded and local experts as possible and in Janet found someone who had all the knowledge we needed but was also a member of our community, located only a short 20 minute drive away.

Next, it would be a good idea to make sure you have a valid Will with Powers of Attorney forms to designate someone to act on your behalf if you are not able or qualified to make decisions regarding your investments and personal care. This means you will need both a good lawyer and that trustworthy individual (your executor) who has some knowledge about your financial affairs or the capacity to learn about them and make reasonable decisions.

The importance of the lawyer cannot be understated. Dying without a valid Will (known as dying Intestate) will impose possible government intervention or worse yet, decisions about the disbursement of your assets that may not match your desires and interests. A lawyer with specialized knowledge in the nature and details of trusts and tax matters would be most helpful, particularly as you build your wealth to avoid leaving a complex mess behind when you're gone.

Are we getting ahead of ourselves? I don't think so.

Even if you feel there's not much "wealth" to structure and protect today, it still makes sense to create the foundation on which you want to build. Especially if you *do* start following some of the paths we traced and include real estate and other non-traditional assets in your financial plan. You will want to be sure your family is protected. Start today, adjust and update tomorrow.

You will no doubt want to speak with a life insurance advisor. You would be best-served to speak with someone who also understands the needs of a more sophisticated investment plan that might include real estate holdings and legal entities you might wish to set up. In fact you should investigate the tax advantages of using life insurance to help you both create and protect your family's legacy. The myriad options may surprise you.

You should make sure your chosen insurance professional is someone you can trust and realizes that they will be but one person on your board of directors. They should be aware they might need to consult with other members of the board (accountant, lawyer etc.) They must understand that your interests are to be served first, that their recommendations need to be an integral part of your overall plan and not stand out as the central star. You could of course say this about everyone you ask to serve on your board.

You also need to recognize that to some degree, your investments will include publically traded securities. Bonds, GICs, mutual funds, Exchange Traded Funds (ETFs) and stocks will play a role in the plan you build. They should however, never be selected to the exclusion and at the expense of other types of assets.

Financial planners and stock brokers will sell you what they are licensed to sell. Rare will be the case that you will find an advisor from the bank, financial planning or investment firm who will speak to you about assets they *do not* sell. This is in part due to the fact they cannot make money on these sales – but just as importantly – they are not licensed to sell nor can they meet compliance rules and regulations required to protect you if they did indeed discuss the other asset classes beyond their capabilities. We will go into the details on these "other assets" as we work through our Catch Up Investing journey together. For now – just hold onto the thought that if all of your investments were held in publically traded securities – there would be absolutely no way to ensure you were adequately if not completely diversified.

A rising tide may lift all boats but a receding tide would be just as dramatic. Wouldn't it make sense for you to have at least a portion of your money invested in something besides a boat; like maybe a mountain chalet or an airplane?

All this aside – you will need an advisor to help you make decisions on how much to invest, where and how. Again, referrals are key. Find out who among your family, friends and external contacts have been successfully investing for years and ask them to introduce you to a professional you can trust. We'll spend more time discussing the selection of this expert board member later along the way in our journey.

If you are going to include non-public assets in your portfolio mix; you would be just as wise to find experts to hold seats on your personal board. These may include an advisor to help you invest in Real Estate, someone licensed to provide you guidance on investing in private equities and a contact that can help you invest in precious metals. Experts in these fields have very highly specialized knowledge.

Finally and more intimately – your Personal Board of Directors will include your spouse, trusted family members (if qualified or at least reasonable thinkers) and friends and contacts who can act as mentors and advisors.

But this is no time to act on faith. Be sure you hold board seats only for people you know for certain who have been successful with longer track records of success than anyone else you may currently know. This means stepping out of your comfort zone to seek out these mentors and mustering up the courage to ask for help.

There is an old expression that implies there is money in every town and on every street. This makes sense, even in the most downtrodden locales. Start your search there and if you find people unaccommodating – then expand your search. You might even come to the conclusion that there are no successful potential directors anywhere in sight. While I don't think this is actually the case – I do have a suggestion.

Exercise your creative mind and your ability to search the Internet. I don't mean read posts and forums on the Internet as we all know the blogosphere is rife with bad advice, malevolent agendas and simply rotten people. Look for training and support centres (yes that's the Canadian spelling) who can offer you the support you need. We'll discuss a few organizations that we consulted that may also be of similar help to you.

As we started our discussion about building your personal board – we acknowledged that you cannot possibly be expected to know everything. The same will be said of your board directors. They may not have all the answers either.

They may make mistakes. Deal with it and understand that making mistakes is part of the learning process. Some mistakes hurt more than others and you'll have to either live with the mistake, hope you can find a way out of the situation you've made for yourself or find a way to mitigate the damages over time.

I know it sounds like I've given you nothing but reasons to throw in the towel and run for the next gallon of Haagen-Dazs and a spoon. There's a method to my madness. While I cannot promise you perfect rainbows and unicorns ahead – I can share with you our experiences The rest of our journey together in the pages that follow, hold more good news than bad.

I do however have a duty to share with you as much as I can in an honest and open dialogue. Even though that dialogue is one-way (unless you can imagine my voice in your head as you read these pages) I am choosing to be as careful and compliant with you and your best interests as possible.

Canadian Eh?

Nothing in this book or on my website (www.catchupinvesting.ca) is meant to elicit a trade or investment of any kind. I am here only to share our journey with you and suggest things you can consider if you need to step outside the ordinary to find the extraordinary. As I help Canadians find advisors who can help them select the best path for them; know these advisors will all be bound by regulatory rules that mandate a responsibility to "know you". This means they will all ask you questions and make suitable recommendations. If they don't – then move on down the road.

Now let's take the first step down that road together.

The Bottom Line:

1. Jay Shetty once said people come into your life for a reason, a season or a lifetime. It might make sense for you to seek out the ones who can help you the most and be patient, candid and caring enough to stick around for a while.

CHAPTER 3

Choosing Between Retirement and Tax-Sheltered Account Alternatives

There are two kinds of small account investors in this World. Well OK – maybe there are many more but for the purposes of this story – let's just say there are two; those who have work pensions with matching contributions and those without. One of these has a clear advantage over the other. Guess.

Publically traded investments or securities can be defined as stocks, bonds, mutual funds, exchange traded funds (ETFs) and GICs or (CDs in the US). They are available for purchase by any member of the public through a variety of distribution channels and intermediaries. These securities can be held in either fully taxable non-registered or tax-sheltered registered accounts. Registered retirement savings accounts in the US principally include 401Ks and IRAs. In Canada, they exist as RRSPs and TFSAs.

For the purposes of our discussion in this chapter we are going to ignore the other kinds of tax-sheltered accounts as right now we are only discussing retirement savings vehicles. Let's return to the point I made above about the two different types of investors. As you started reading this chapter – I'd be willing to bet you immediately identified the camp to which *you* belong.

What is the role of a tax-sheltered retirement savings account? Your 401K or RRSP is meant to shelter pre-tax dollars by making a deposit in an account, to grow free of taxation and one day, create a stream of taxable income when you retire. In a perfect World, you make sound decisions today and will hopefully find yourself in a lower tax bracket when it comes time to start taking that income. Tax deferral does not equate to tax avoidance.

Let's now consider what kinds of market returns are possible and then the broader "art of the possible".

For the sake of argument let's say you've constructed a balanced portfolio with a publically traded investment mix of 60% equities and 40% bonds of various lengths in term. Let's further assume that the long term returns (including interest and dividends) for this kind of allocation are between 6% and 8.0%. Of course there are no guarantees that these returns are sustainable indefinitely. But let's say for the sake of argument those kinds of returns are achievable as they have been in the past, for as long as you need. The question then becomes, could you do better elsewhere? Perhaps.

Private equity investments are generally available with target returns of between 12% and 15% annually. Some are even constructed with targeted returns in excess of 20% annually although they do come with higher degrees of risk. We'll explore all these private equity investments shortly. For now – just consider the numbers and know that a similar 60% equity and 40% income type portfolio, including private equities could yield returns in excess of 16%. The answer to the question we asked earlier is – yes – there might be investments where you could do better.

The bottom line is this; if you work for an employer that equally (or even partially) matches your retirement account Contributions, your 8% return is automatically enhanced and perhaps as much as doubled at no cost to you. If your employer does support you with matching Contributions, the decision to take advantage of your work-sponsored retirement program seems pretty obvious. If you are not lucky enough to benefit from one of these work-sponsored retirement 401K and RRSP accounts then all is not lost. The decision in that case rests on how much you earn and your current age.

If you are a relatively high income earner, then saving in a retirement account that resides outside the workplace may still pay off for you if your Contributions will lower your income enough to fall into a lower tax bracket, today. The market returns in this case might be enough for you to make that deposit and hopefully manage the account's growth so you can build your retirement nest-egg.

The other consideration is age. The closer you are to 40 – the better off you might be in maximizing your savings in a registered retirement savings account using pre-tax dollars.

If you have no employer matching benefit and if you could do better by choosing private equity investment vehicles outside the range available in any public securities based retirement account, then you might be better off skipping the pre-tax dollar accounts (401 K and RRSP) in favor of tax-sheltered growth accounts that are funded with **after-tax dollars**. In The US these include IRAs and in Canada, the Tax-Free Savings Account or TFSA.

Governments in both countries afford their citizens with the facility to invest after-tax dollars that are left free to grow in a tax-sheltered account and withdraw the funds when needed down the road without paying tax on exit.

These fully tax-sheltered accounts may provide the investor with a vehicle to hold private equities that grow over time at an accelerated rate. You would be wise to research the ability to hold private equities in work-sponsored AND non-work sponsored retirement accounts.

The Bottom Line:

1. If you have a work sponsored Pension Plan or Group Retirement savings vehicle with matched contributions – you would do well to participate.

2. If you have no such work-sponsored plan – then the question becomes that of considering your current earnings and the need to manage your declared income as a contribution might drop you into a lower income tax bracket.

3. If you have no such work-sponsored plan, then your next consideration is which investment vehicles you should

choose; public vs private and where to invest. If private equities have greater promise – then choose them over public. If you can hold private equities in an individual registered retirement savings account (401K or RRSP) then that is your next best option. If you cannot – then look to invest these sums in an after-tax dollar sheltered account such as an IRA or TFSA.

4. If you are closer to Age 40 – then you should build your individual and or work-sponsored accounts, first.

5. If you truly believe you will still be in a high tax bracket in retirement because your income will still demand that level of taxation, then you should opt for the IRA and TFSA freedom of earning tax-free growth and taking tax-free income.

It's just math.

CHAPTER 4

Private Equities

First, I have a word to share with you up front. Throughout this chapter and the rest of the book and our journey together – I will use the terms "exempt market" and "private equity" markets almost interchangeably. I may use the terms as root-words to describe securities, products and projects. You'll get the hang of it as you read on from here.

One of the first lessons we hear from investment advisors is the importance of diversification. It is funny how that has come to mean "buy as many different mutual funds from me as possible – and you'll be 'diversified'". If you have nothing but mutual funds and other banking and stock market products – you have effectively created portfolio "diworsification" and are taking on more risk than you need.

Here's the thing.

Bankers and investment advisors are paid to sell. In order to create the safest portfolio possible – they will try to mitigate risk by selling you products that might not behave exactly alike in any given market. Bonds are meant to cushion the blow of any dramatic changes in the stock market but are themselves prone to wild market fluctuations when interest rates and market sentiment rise and fall.

The problem is – these investment products are all traded actively in the market, every day the market is open. The stock and bond markets are not only a reflection of the strength of the underlying quality of that investment – but also a reflection of investor sentiment. If there is one certainty (beyond death and taxes) it's that most investors really aren't "Investors". We tend to be savers of convenience and rather poor ones at that.

Have you ever wondered why investment advisors never talk to you about precious metals (real and not in mutual funds or exchange traded funds), real estate (again, real properties, not just funds, exchange traded funds or stocks) and other non-traditional investments? It's simple – it's because they don't get paid and can't meet regulatory requirements that grant them the safety to provide advice.

Fear as in "False Evidence Appearing Real" moves most of us to buy when it appears to be safe to buy (when markets achieve "highs" that are way too expensive) and sell when the market appears to be risky (when the market is "tanking" and really *not* safe). Warren Buffet said – "Buy when others are fearful and Sell when others are greedy. Few of us actually take that advice. We are motivated by greed and the fear of missing out (FOMO) and buy or we panic and do precisely the wrong thing at the wrong time by selling.

There are so many good lessons and sage advice from which to learn in addition to Buffet's words included above. They include: "The smart money always invests in trying times" and "In crisis and danger lie opportunity". Small business owners and savvy investors live their lives by these words. They run counter-intuitive to what you think you should do and are seldom wrong.

Consider how many of these small and medium sized business owners exist and create wealth in your neighbourhood? Look at how well they live and yet also manage their money well? What would it be like to walk in their shoes and enjoy the benefits of the wealth they created? You can!

Beyond the obvious reasons including hard work and making more good decisions than bad, it takes patience and the idea that wealth creation is not an overnight event. They hang on in bad times as well as enjoy the good. You may not have had this long-term view in mind in the past and it may be what has been holding you back; like it did, me.

But we're talking about "Catch-Up-Investing" here and there is a way you can benefit from these "smart neighbours" of yours and do it within a reasonable time frame.

These small to medium sized entrepreneurs seek financing to build their active businesses, resource exploration and extraction projects and real estate developments. In each case, an investment is structured to meet the needs of a company or particular venture. These projects are securitized as an investment product, described in a document called an "Offering memorandum" and sold to individual and sometimes institutional investors. These investment products are designed and offered by exempt market dealers (EMDs) and collectively make up what we call the "Private Equity or Capital Market".

There are restrictions as to who can invest and how much they can commit. The rules are somewhat but not entirely different in The US than in Canada. Income, net worth and past experience usually drives your ability to participate. In many cases the sheer size of the minimum investment is enough to keep out those who should not dare to partake.

Accredited Investors are those with substantial net worth and or liquid assets – and/or with consistent individual incomes of $200,000 annually or $300,000 annually when combined with a spouse. These investors can secure positions in most private securities for positions of $25,000. Several more exclusive equities require commitments of $250,000 per position and perhaps more.

In Ontario in 2016 the rules became a little more relaxed when the average investor who earns at least $75,000 was cleared to invest up to $10,000 annually in any one or combination of private equity strategies. Households earning at least $125,000 between 2 spouses are now allowed to invest up to $30,000 or even $100,000 annually, provided they have completed know-your-client due diligence interviews and received guidance from an exempt market dealer "representative" (EMDR).

The Ontario rules were very quickly adopted across Canada and American readers would do well to consult professional private equity advisors near them to determine options available in their market.

🍁 Canadian Eh?

Here is a little-known secret just for a very limited set of Canadian investors. As I mentioned to you – I used to work on Bay Street as a licensed Financial Advisor. That lofty title meant I was a formerly licensed and registered securities advisor who bought and sold public market securities for clients and my own account. Currently registered or retired advisors can qualify to invest as if they were fully Accredited Investors and take advantage of the most exciting projects at the lowest possible levels (at the discretion of the issuer).

When my wife and I were starting over, we certainly did not qualify as Accredited Investors anew and would not be where we are today without having this inside access. The good news is that with the new rule changes – ANY investor can qualify and participate to some degree as long as they are careful and receive adequate guidance.

This provides you as the average "Catch Up Investor" with greater options should you wish to restructure your investments or find ways to take advantage of other Catch-Up strategies in your registered and non-registered accounts.

What sets these investments apart from normal publically traded securities like stocks, bonds and funds is the fact they are usually not liquid (although the recent rule changes and product designs offered by some EMDs have made some of these investment products available with an early-exit facility (at a cost) but are usually held until the project is complete. Once complete – investors will receive their projected returns, acknowledging up front that these returns are not guaranteed.

This lack of liquidity can be considered a "good thing". If there is one common trait among most individual investors is; we often do the wrong thing at the wrong time. We water our weeds and pick our flowers. We buy 'high" and sell "low". We invest with too much or too little risk. We don't allocate our investments appropriately to our time horizons nor do we recognize the fact we even *have* a time horizon. We don't meet with our advisors regularly to rebalance our portfolios or check in to see if our plans are on track; if we have a plan at all. In short – we're a mess.

Allocating some of our investments to private equities helps us (as in my wife and I) maintain a sense of discipline and avoid all the noise from market pundits and prognosticators who would have us sell when we should buy, buy when we should sell and buy indiscriminately.

The objective of each private equity security is different as would be the case for any product sold in the public markets. Some products are designed to provide regular income and some are built to achieve long term growth. Many vehicles are structured to provide both yield and growth.

This makes sense in that private businesses build their companies to generate income today and provide the growth needed to fund expansion and a stronger foundation for the company's future. These investment products are funded by investors like you to make this possible and your reward for accepting this risk is the projected return. For a more graphic illustration, please visit my website at www.catchupinvesting.ca. There you will find a short video clip provided courtesy of the Private Client Markets Association that should clear up any questions.

Private equity investments include real estate projects oriented towards new construction, redevelopment, long term rentals and purpose specific projects like building or operating students and senior's residences. In those cases where rental properties are involved there is usually a regularly recurring revenue stream of between 6% - 12% as well as price appreciation as the values of the underlying buildings increase over time. The objective is to increase the value of the property and increase rents by beautifying and upgrading the properties and or normalizing the rents collected to a more uniform amount. At some point, targets are achieved and the project may be prepared for exit, or held for the long term.

Other real estate projects are designed to provide developers with the capital they need to secure lands on which they build condominiums, low rise and individual housing and mixed use buildings that combine several types of residential and commercial buildings in a single project. These are usually term-specific projects that exit when the development or building is fully populated with unit owners and all profits to developers and investors alike have been distributed.

Total target annualized returns for income generating equities lie between 8% - 15% and somewhere between 20% - 25% for construction private equity projects. We have barely broken even on some of the deals we bought and have been delighted to rake-in returns in excess of 40% on others. Please do not look at the outliers as being normal – you could lose.

Your challenge is to find the best overall investment options in either the public or private markets. It's becoming more challenging every year. While the embedded costs in mutual funds are coming down in Canada – they are still quite high with many mutual funds costing between 2% - 3%. Stock market returns over the past few years have been quite strong but are they sustainable? Index funds have been great at delivering good returns that have beaten the performance of the majority of active money managers – at much lower cost but, will that too change in the future? Perhaps it makes sense to include both active and passive strategies in your investment mix? You could include passive index fund and ETF options and then add private equities to enhance your overall returns.

You could look at income oriented private equities to enhance your fixed income returns but would be wise to consider them as an "equity" investment given their higher risk profile. Look for private equities that participate in pay-day loan financing and Mortgage Investment Corporations (MICs). You might also consider finding ways to be an investment lender in the private mortgage market. There are several opportunities in both the US and Canada to participate in all these markets, earning better-than-public-market rates of return. A good private equity advisor or EMDR can help you navigate the waters to help you find your best options.

Canadian Eh?

Some exempt products (usually at the accredited level) require set-up costs such as the construction of a selling centre in the case of a condominium or housing project. These invested amounts represent losses for tax purposes and the investors are allocated a proportional amount of that total they may in turn use to offset earned income when preparing their annual taxes.

Here comes that disclosure statement again. Readers – do your homework and consult with your accountant to see what if any options apply in your case. Canadians who invest in qualifying projects will be issued a T 5013 form to report losses in the case of partnership losses.

Private equity investments also include operating companies that rely on real estate for the structure on which those businesses operate. These include short and long term storage facilities which take advantage of the need to compensate for the ever-shrinking footprint of today's condominium units and operating businesses like car washes and laundromats. In each case, the land is a central tenet on which the business is based but the operation (renting storage space or providing services like car washes) keeps the customers coming in the door.

You would also do well to consider private equity deals that feature water resource allocation and unit ownership in farmland projects (more on these later) that represent ownership in scarce resources with known future demand. The World needs water and food. It makes sense to look to that scarcity for some very healthy returns especially since those returns have little if any correlation at all to whatever happens on Wall Street or Bay Street.

Private equity investments are structured either as limited partnerships or as mutual fund trusts. They are almost always structured with total financing requirements. Once reached – or sold out – that's it. The issue is closed and investors who wanted "in" are shut out and forced to wait for the next new project coming down the road.

My wife and I have experienced these over-subscribed markets and have been forced to wait for the "next one". So my best advice is to speak to an exempt or private equity advisor and find out what kinds of projects resonate best with you and then act fast and commit when your advisor calls. Please read that sentence again as I never said "rush in and don't do your homework".

The good news with these products is that the structures are usually cookie-cutter like and are used over and over again on different projects. Once you understand the risks and the way the security behaves – the easier it is to consider the specific differences which are usually defined by location and the other unique qualities that should all be specified in the Offering Memorandum we mentioned a moment ago. Get it. Read it.

The Bottom Line:

1. There are way too many kinds of private equity to mention

2. They all carry different levels of income and potential for capital gains

3. They are structured either as limited partnerships or mutual fund trusts with different rights and restrictions

4. Target returns are very attractive and range widely from 8% to 25%. They come with different liquidity restrictions and degrees of risk.

5. There are income restrictions although there is likely some way that every investor can participate.

6. An advisor is required and a key part of your Personal Board of Directors. Find one you trust, listen to them and consider their advice before making any decisions

That gives us a pretty good high level understanding of private equities. Now that we have a handle on private equities – let's quickly examine your available options in the public markets as you should consider including both "privates" and "publics" in your Catch Up Investing strategy.

CHAPTER 5

And Your Advisor Is?

After having shared a one-sided opinion about the public markets, you might consider why we've included public securities in our Catch-Up Investing program at all. Recognizing that the public markets are subject to insider trading abuse, market manipulation, institutional trading domination and market pundits who always seem to argue both sides at the same time; it would be understandable if you thought we hated the public markets. That is simply not the case and I can assure you that stocks, mutual funds, exchange traded funds, bonds and treasuries are some of our most favorite things. I just make sure they are not the *only* things we use to build our family's future financial security.

My goal for this chapter is not to spend a great deal of time defining what each of these publically traded securities are but to share my thoughts with you as to what the differences are between service providers and advisors and to help guide you on your journey.

Please read the following chapter as my opinion only. Your experience and observations may be quite different.

Financial Planners and Stock Brokers

Financial Planners in Canada may not be registered nor is there any set qualification standard to call yourself a "financial planner", although that may soon change. Having said that, the vast majority of planners are conscientious professionals who consider the advice their clients require first and the products they provide, second. Financial planners are often restricted as to the types of products they are approved to sell, depending on how they are registered (if at all) and the level of training they have received. Planners may work for small investment firms, banks, bank-owned securities firms or larger independent investment firms.

There are many service and income models in the financial planning market. Fee for service or "fee only" planners make their money by creating for their clients, specific financial and investment plans. They are paid either a flat fee or annual charge per service or per hour and sometimes receive recurring revenue by billing their clients additionally for each hour spent rendering advice or investing clients' funds. Their products are usually restricted to some or all of stocks, bonds, mutual funds and GICs, although may include life insurance products if they are dual licensed.

Fee only planners may represent your best deal as long as you make sure the planner receives no income for products sold unless such income is disclosed in advance. This ensures that you and your planner are always on the same page and win together.

Stock brokers are licensed to sell all investment products but require separate and additional licensing to sell life insurance, Options (contracts that give you the choice to buy or sell securities without obligation that can protect investors from down side risk, create additional income and or afford investors the ability to buy securities at more favorable pricing by paying fees up front) and or Commodities (grains, metals etc.). It may be just a hunch of mine but, if you are trying "Catch Up" then you likely don't have an immediate need for either Options or Commodities in your portfolio – or at least you probably don't have that need, today. Don't lose focus.

Be sure to look for professional accreditation and an advisor you can trust. But where do you find them and what should you consider?

In short, financial advisors work at banks, credit unions, financial planning firms and securities firms that are both independent and bank owned. If they *are not* fee-only planners – then they rely on receiving a portion of the commissions and fees generated from the products they sell you. They are required to make "suitable" recommendations but not necessarily promote your "best" option. That mitigates their risk but exposes you potentially to the risk there might be something better for you out there. Be sure to understand what fees are built into or on top of any products recommended and ask for everything in writing. Read what you are given and ask questions.

Financial planners and stock brokers who work for large investment firms, independent and bank owned stock brokerages are also paid based on how much they sell. Whenever a sale is made, they too receive a portion of the total commission you pay. This may depend on the type of firm with which you are dealing. Securities firms have higher overhead costs than do financial planning firms. The same could be said for large national firms vs. privately held smaller firms.

This portion is referred to as the "payout". The more the advisor sells in aggregate to all the clients they manage over the course of the year; the higher their payout. The size of the payout is also dictated by the size of the firm, the services offered to advisors and the firm's overhead. This all creates something of a sliding scale which defines how much advisors are paid is itself referred to as "the grid".

New investment advisors and those who do not meet sales targets may receive as little as 20% of the total commission you pay. The rest goes to the house. As you can imagine – it might be tough to make a living when the payout is so low. Top sales reps may clear as much as 50% of the total commission on the grid. The smaller the firm – and the more securities a rep sells; the higher the potential is their payout. Some firms maximize the payout but charge a ticket fee for every security bought or sold.

Over the past 15 years, the stark payout splits have resulted in the formation of a team selling approach where new planners can be mentored by more seasoned professionals. This is likely a good thing but the fact remains – you might just be another means to a paycheque (again with the Canadian spelling).

One of the results of all this is the fact that financial advisor's "books" (the total amount of all client monies managed by them) must be forever growing in order to achieve and maintain the top levels of payout on the grid. If the team's (or individual rep's) sales slip – so will their payout. This begets a cycle of production where teams must keep finding more clients and grow larger by adding more sales reps, selling opportunities by offering new products or suffer a possible cutback in aggregate income. This doesn't work so well for teams with high staff counts and costs.

I suppose this is better than the way it was when I was a licensed advisor. Back in the 1990's, I often saw advisors managing books of less than $15.0 Million in assets under administration and making President's Club award levels for sales generating in excess of $750,000 in annual commissions.

I saw a number of advisors conduct inappropriate buying and selling of the investments in client accounts in order to meet higher payout thresholds. This practice is known as "churning" and should seem self-evident as being unscrupulous to you. Today – advisors require books of business well in excess of $75.0 - $100.0 Million in total assets to come close to those levels of sales. This was one of the biggest reasons why I left the business back in 2004. I couldn't stand seeing the kind of client abuse (which was minimal in terms of the numbers of reps but maximum in terms of the damage done to everyone's reputation) that seemed to "come to life" on the front page of many of the country's newspapers each and every day.

Private and Discretionary Asset Managers and Counsel Firms

Somewhere above the fray lies a set of investment professionals that have evolved beyond the ordinary advisor. These women and men charge fees to manage assets and earn status as Portfolio Managers, or PMs. Their task lists include getting to know their clients, documenting goals and making suitable investment recommendations. They have wide latitude however and unlike conventional advisors need not seek permission or approval to make individual buying or selling trades. They have full freedom or discretion to act independently.

In the spirit of full disclosure, I am happy to share with you my wife and I use the services of a private investment counsellor or "PM". I have known Richard since 1992. He was responsible for recruiting me into the investment industry and still has our complete confidence today. He is one of the mentors I mentioned in my Dedication at the front of this book.

"Rick" works with our family, managing accounts for my mother, brother and my immediate family, consisting of my wife and daughter. Rick works with individual stocks, bonds, funds and writes Option trades for us to generate additional income. He has full discretionary rights to manage our funds, although he and I are in regular contact and because of our history and my background, discuss most trades and strategies.

Some of you may be asking why as a former investment professional, I work with another advisor? The answer is really quite simple. My current job responsibilities have just been increased and I no longer have as much time as I would like to spend on our investments. Add to that, Rick has been working with my family for many years and he also provides a margin of safety for my wife Susan, should anything happen to me. I guess you could say the family recruited Rick to be on our collective Family Board of Directors.

Rick's model is "high touch". He charges a flat percentage of assets to service our account and an extremely small fee of pennies per share to trade securities. Every deal is different. Some discretionary managers may charge an additional performance fee. This fee is only charged if the manager is able to beat the previous high-water mark (total account value in dollars) and will not apply if they fail to beat that target.

It might occur that the previous high water mark is unbeatable meaning the performance fee is not collected for several years. Combine this with the fact that discretionary managers often charge fees much lower than conventional investment advisors and the end-result is greater alignment. We have found a great deal of comfort knowing we are saving fees and working with someone we trust who will never "win" at our expense. Being on the same page with our advisor is what matters most.

Discretionary managers charge fees based on the size of the account and frequently limit taking on accounts with less than $250,000 in total investment assets and sometimes more. Fees (before performance fees described earlier) run anywhere from 0.75% - 1.5% - and perhaps less, depending on account size.

And yet there may be even less costly ways to engage a private asset manager without having to turn over complete control on trading decisions. In fact these asset managers avoid making any trading recommendations at all.

Some private asset managers work primarily with Exchange Traded Funds (ETFs) which are passive market securities. These single securities trade like stocks on the World's major markets and either emulate a market index (TSX, Dow Jones Industrial Index etc.) similar to index mutual funds or they may represent a unique selection of market stocks that are fixed into a single trading vehicle. The main appeal of these ETFs is lower costs.

Because these are passive investments, trading costs are minimized. This results in lower trading fees, capital gains and internally generated capital gains taxes. The end result is your accounts will attract much lower overall costs. Often – these passively managed fund arrangements can be set up to manage accounts of $75,000 to well over $1.0 Million. Accounts are usually balanced at the end of the year to make sure the investor's questionnaire-determined and recommended asset mix is brought back into proportion.

I believe it is possible to create a hybrid account using a combination of both passive ETFs and more aggressive private equities. This unique combination recognizes the fact that many if not most active managers fail to beat their respective target market indexes. So wouldn't it naturally make sense to overweight passively managed ETFs that meet the market and add (to whatever degree you like) more aggressive investments to add performance?

OK – so here it comes again. Past performance is no guarantee of future performance and investors need to recognize they are assuming greater risk in the private markets. I do believe however that the past can be an indication of what may be possible and that an allocation of between 10.0% and 30.0% of your total portfolio into private equities, with targeted annualized returns in excess 9.0% may indeed be worthy of your consideration.

Even though some of the private equities may be structured to generate regular income like a bond – I suggest you consider them as equities and make them a part of your portfolio only within the confines of the portion of your account that you've reserved for equity investments.

Balance is the thing here.

Next – let's spend some time discussing true "Catch-Up" strategies, namely Real Estate; why it is such a strong option for you to consider and why we chose to make it a central part of our own program.

The Bottom Line:

1. Even a well-diversified portfolio constructed entirely of publically traded securities is not truly diversified.

2. Securities recommended and sold as "suitable" by advisors may not always be your best options.

3. Securities can be purchased within mutual funds, ETFs or individually and sold by commission-paid, fee only or private asset managers. They can be selected with your participation or entirely by your advisor or portfolio manager in a discretionary account. Fees and responsibilities differ.

Canadian Eh?

Should you wish to learn more about private asset managers who specialize in active and or passive money management, we may be able to help answer your questions.

CHAPTER 6

Real Estate

You may have heard that more millionaires have been created by investing in real estate than in any other way. My wife and I believe this to be true. For us, real estate is what we chose to develop a retirement income and pension substitute to augment our savings.

I never worked for a company that offered a pension plan; until very recently. I am grateful for the fact I now work for a company that supports their employees by matching staff contributions with an equal sum, up to a very generous amount each year. My wife retired some 5 years ago and enjoys a fully defined benefit pension and so we determined we would have to create a pension plan of sorts for me to help equate our incomes in retirement.

Up until 10-12 years ago, I had failed to build much of a RRSP. In fact whatever was there had been liquidated in order to support the struggling business I mentioned at the beginning of the book. This seemed like the only "way out"

at the time but in hind-sight was one of the very worse financial decisions I ever made.

The idea of using real estate to create my "pension" was borne out of my having read Robert Kiyosaki's book "Rich Dad – Poor Dad". Perhaps the greatest revelation in that book and throughout his many books was the true definition of an "asset".

An asset is something you own or control that produces income; period.

An asset is not a lump of something that sits there and loses value. At best, cars, boats and campers can be tools that are used on the job or for fun. More often than not – they're just toys. In fact (and this concept blew my mind) your house is not in and of itself an asset, either.

If you're lucky – your home will have appreciated in value over the many years you've dutifully paid your mortgage. You could pay off any remaining mortgage and downsize to a smaller dwelling when the kids are grown and gone. If the mortgage has been paid off, the resulting cash could be significant. But you still need a place to live. Buying a smaller home or renting become your immediately available options. You could of course also look to relocate to a cheaper jurisdiction at home or abroad and live off the income produced by investing everything. These strategies have merit but delay the creation of income and wealth until some point down the road.

The problem with waiting is uncertainty. Who knows what your home will be worth in the future? Will the market be strong or will it be in decline? What investment options will be available to you at some point down the road when you are ready to act? Perhaps that's too much uncertainty.

What is the flip-side of that coin?

Take action, today.

Money tied up in your personal residence won't create value for you unless you tap its unrealized potential. There's an old physics lesson in there; something about the stationary object that stays stationary producing no energy vs. an object in motion. Guess where the action lies?

There are costs and risks in investing. There are also unknown risks and costs that you may never even recognize but none-the-less face when you do nothing. These risks are known as the "Opportunity Cost" which means the penalty your future will face should you sit and do nothing. You have to embrace the idea of "what could be" just as much as rationalizing the apparent risks of being stuck in the unappealing World of "what is".

For us, the appeal of real estate investing was the cash-flow produced each and every month and the prospects of having a tenant (or client as we've come to call them) pay down our mortgage. The idea of capital appreciation as prices go up over time is nice but icing on the cake. We like *cake* and for us that's regular, monthly income.

Monthly rents should increase annually over time like everything else. Rising property values give you the opportunity to access some of your growing equity and finance more properties. That line of thinking is great if you're out to build an empire and continually add to your holdings. That was never the case for us. We simply wanted to create a base level income, roughly equal in size to my wife's pension and augment that by continuing to work in some capacity, add income from registered and non-registered investments and our government pensions. We have a target level of income that we are trying to achieve and with divine intervention, good planning and a little luck, we should meet those goals.

It's at this point I always like to share the "giggles" that overcome me whenever I read an article about an investment advisor who states categorically how much better off people would be if they only invested in the stock market and ignore real estate. Talk about a biased position!

The evidence they share is that the average price of a typical house, duplex or condo appreciates only 3.0% annually. Let's ignore major markets like Toronto and Vancouver which have seen price spikes well in excess of these levels. These markets might be considered as over-heated and may just as likely come back down to Earth. The figures for other markets in Canada and the US exhibit more reasonable annual price-growth figures annually; so let's stay with those. The stock market, in contrast boasts long term total returns of between 6.0% and 8.0%. Both figures are reported net of inflation. So on the face of our stock expert's opinion – he or she might be right.

Let's leave out the impact of taxation right now as there are pros and cons to both strategies depending on how esoteric and complete you want to make the analysis. Take for now taxation is a bit of a wash.

Let's evaluate.

The true power of investing in real estate is again the magic of someone else paying down your mortgage. A home that costs $300,000 may cost nothing up front (if you use a HELOC to provide the down payment) and may produce as much as $1,800 monthly or $21,600 annually.

Using a mortgage rate of 3%, a 5-Year fixed term and 25 Year amortization (for illustration purposes) – the costs to carry the full mortgage cost of that property is $1,420. Add property tax of about $200 per month and a little insurance of another $125 and you are still net cash-flow positive $55.00 each month. Okay – so no-one is getting rich here – at least not quickly. But it costs you nothing to get into the game except accepting the risk of making a decision and perhaps a catastrophic market reversal.

You might have additional costs to carry if you go without rent for 1-2 months or if you need to make repairs but the math is simple. Over time your mortgage will be paid with someone else's money and you've manufactured a "theoretically infinite return" by accepting the risk AND used no money of your own to create your own future.

Now let's assume you actually have the 20% needed for a down payment in cash. The math also looks bright. On a $300,000 property – your carrying costs would be a lower cost mortgage of $1,136 plus again the same $200 per month property tax and $125 insurance. Your cash flow has just increased by the difference in mortgage payments; or $339 per month. This ends up returning to you $4,068 annually, roughly comparable to a dividend of 6.8% ($4,068 on your $60,000 down payment). That means your total return is

6.8% plus 3% (in average price appreciation) for a total return of 9.8% annually.

Safe to say – both options may make sense depending on your ability to step ever so slightly outside your comfort zone and consider that there's more to life than just stocks, bonds and mutual funds.

Let's dig deeper.

I mentioned a few minutes ago that the beauty of real estate investing was the fact we were servicing our mortgage payment with someone else's money. You may be familiar with the term "leverage" or "other people's money". These concepts are universal to pretty much any line of investing and may create some tax advantages as the interest costs may be tax-deductible.

When applying the concept of leverage to investing in real estate – you can finance 100% of the purchase price (or purchase down payment) using a HELOC or 80% of the price if you have the cash available. That means you could be financing using (at "worse" if you follow my drift) $4 of someone else's money for every $1 you commit from your own funds. Why; because banks and finance companies love property. There is always an asset to seize should you fail to pay and the values are not nearly as likely to fall as far and as fast as securities might the stock market.

Our stock advisor friend may be able to open up a margin account and provide you with 1:1 matching where the investment company will loan you $1 for every $1 you commit from your own bank account. You might be able to find more generous terms.

While it is obvious that the greater amount of leverage brings an additional element of risk – it does present an additional opportunity for growth. My wife and I decided, that was a risk worth taking as we believe people always need a place to live while they might not always benefit from a basket of stocks and funds that could contain the next "Nortel".

Digging still deeper; let's consider the alternatives of investing $60,000 (same size as your down payment) in the stock market using your own funds.

Assuming the upper growth total return target we cited earlier of 8% in the stock market and ignoring costs and taxes, your $60,000 nest egg could grow to $129,535 in 10 years. That represents a total net return of $69,535 or 115.8% of your original invested capital. Great!

Now let's consider your rental property option and that same $60,000 to invest. The house you purchase, growing at 3.0% annually grows to $403,174. Your equity position has increased by $103,174 as someone else paid down your mortgage; but what about that $220,000 mortgage? Let's assume you elected to take a 30 year amortization (if available) instead of a conventional 25 year. The only reason I'm suggesting that is to make the math easier in our example and for no other reason.

Given that – your $220,000 mortgage will have been paid down by fully one third of the face amount in the same 10 year period we used to evaluate the stock investment. You will have generated an additional $73,333 in equity – just by holding onto the property and having someone else make the payments.

Next – let's recall the positive monthly cash flow we identified in our example of $339 a month. Over ten years (or a total of 120 months) – you would have realized an additional $40,680. But even that's not the end of the story as monthly rents by and large tend to go up over time. Not being greedy – let's assume an annual increase in rent of 2.0%, which is consistent with many rent-controlled jurisdictions. The math gets a little tricky here.

$4,068 ($339 x 12) increasing 2.0% per year for 10 years is $45,434.33 in total increasing rent, collected.

Let's add this all up.

Stocks	$60,000 invested
Total Return	8.0%
Total Value 10 Yrs	$129,535
Net return	$ 69,535
ROE	115.8%

Let's now consider a higher rate of return in the stock market of say, 10%

Stocks	$60,000 invested	
Total Return	10.0%	
Total Value 10 Yrs	$155,625	
Net return	$ 95,625	
ROE	159.4%	($95,625/$60,000)

Now let's look at the rental property option:

Rental Property	$60,000 invested
Value of Property	$300,000
Value in 10 Yrs	$403,174
Equity Difference	$103,174
Mortgage Equity	$ 73,333
Cash flow Received	$ 45,434
Total Net Return	$ 221,941
ROE	369.9% ($221,941/$60,000)

Now remember – this is just an illustration. Returns are not guaranteed and we did not factor in taxes in either scenario. We also declined to include more esoteric accounting strategies such as taking accumulated capital depreciation. This practice affords investors the chance to write off or depreciate the value of their properties over time to defer the taxes owed on rental incomes received. My wife and never did that and to this day pay income taxes as we earn each and every dollar, annually.

We could take the depreciation and defer the taxes owed until such time as we either sell the property or trigger some other kind of tax declaration or disposition. As I am still working and make decent money today – we felt it unwise to defer taxes and make life more difficult on our kids when we're both gone by leaving them with a huge tax bill. It's a matter of personal choice and we do indeed realize that we may be paying more tax today than if we defer.

Ask your accountant as they may advise you differently.

The point I'm trying to make here is that you need to be very wary of the so-called market expert who says real estate investing will never beat time in the stock market. I think you'll agree that appears to be a misleading and biased opinion. Make your decision based on what you can see and figure it out for yourself.

Suffice to say – care and due diligence is required in both investing scenarios and you might include both strategies (Stocks AND Real Estate) as we have. Hopefully, we've now put that argument to bed once and for all.

The Bottom Line:

1. Investing in Real Estate can be structured to create the pension you don't have or haven't built.

2. Real Estate investing is a good alternative and or addition to your investments in public markets.

3. The argument for stocks vs real estate is often biased and not fully explained or understood.

But how do you *really* get started? Well first – you turn the page.

CHAPTER 7

Starting Your Real Estate Investing Adventure

We have already spent enough time discussing the need to have ready cash or tap into the un-used equity in your principal residence (or cottage for that matter). Now let's assemble a check list of sorts as to the rest of the items you need to consider and the members you need to add to your Personal Board of Directors (identified earlier on our Catch Up Investing journey) and why you need them.

Education:

For us, it all started at a real estate investing trade show at a convention centre located near the Toronto International Airport. Four thousand like-minded investors, both new and experienced attended this conference to learn more about making money in real estate. A trade show accompanied some fascinating presentations and I must admit I was a little overwhelmed. I did however come away with two material pieces of immediate knowledge.

First – we learned that we knew absolutely nothing about investing in real estate. Second – we found our first investment strategy; but more about that later. Right now I want to share with you the fact that you need to learn as much as you possibly can before you commit to your first property.

 Canadian Eh?

There are a number of dedicated resources for Canadian Real Estate investors. These include:

REIN:

The Real Estate Investment Network (www.reincanada.com) is a network of investing experts who offer education and training, presenting every possible strategy to support Canadians interested in building a future for themselves in rental properties. The network offers web-based, live and online training. They publish an insightful and resource-packed monthly magazine and support investors with highly-detailed reports to help select the right properties in the right markets. In short, REIN is a resource Canadian investors should make their first call.

The help doesn't end there. They provide advice on bookkeeping and accounting, legal issues like incorporation and help with answering your questions on financing. Membership is offered via a good-better-best structure and can be paid monthly or annually. An innovative property insurance offer is made available by a leading Western Canadian brokerage who has constructed a unique protection product that cannot be found anywhere else. This product indemnifies against vandalism by disgruntled tenants, loss of income and support to bring properties up to today's code if discrepancies to current building codes are discovered when repairs or renovations are required. The coverage is not cheap but is very much in balance with the value built into each policy.

Keyspire:

Keyspire is another Canadian investment network that offers training and support for individuals who want to build a portfolio of rental properties. What makes them different is that while REIN teaches about investing techniques, Keyspire will from time-to-time offer actual investment products. Keyspire also requires an up-front membership fee which may be a roadblock for some.

Keyspire is fronted by a well-known renovation TV personality, Scott McGillvray from Homes and Garden TV (HGTV) Canada. He may even be known to some American viewers as his show is also broadcasted on the DIY Network, South of the border. McGillvray has long been a proponent of real estate investing and the inclusion of income suites to help make property ownership affordable.

In his TV show "Income Property", McGillvray interviews a young couple, family or parent with young or adult child who are facing either some kind of financial hardship or need to find an affordable home in which to live. Scott appears as the 'good guy and financial guru" he seems to be and helps these people make ends meet. The solution is always the inclusion of an income suite of some sort in a basement apartment to help produce the shortfall needed to cover the "uncoverable" mortgage payment and save the day.

Canadian Real Estate Wealth Magazine:

Canadian Real Estate Wealth Magazine (or CREW) is published nine times per year by Key Media and available by subscription or at your local news stand. Full disclosure; I have had the privilege of writing for CREW for the past 15 months. I am not paid for my articles. I do however; believe CREW is one of the best resources available for Canadian investors without initiation fees available at a reasonable subscription fee or competitive price at your local news stand.

CREW provides daily email news updates on the state of the industry and economy. The stories are focused on providing advice and sharing success stories from those who have built larger portfolios of single, multi-family and commercial properties. Professional mortgage brokers and real estate coaches also contribute articles and the feature stories on markets of various sizes, by province are essential reading.

In short CREW has become my go-to resource for initial high-level market screening and insight into what affects us the most.

There are myriad resources available to Canadian property investors. Now let's consider some resources that are widely available for everyone else.

I am quite certain there are training and coaching resources available in every market around the World. You need only do the research to determine the model you wish to pursue and then search for the best teacher possible. Obviously – you would do well to avoid the charlatans and hucksters of the past and look for reviews. Better yet – get involved in some online and in-person support groups. Take courses and start networking with people like you and find them in the classroom (in-person or virtual) or in the conference hall. There's an old saying "shy sales people have skinny kids" We learned the same could be said for real estate investors.

Specifically – we read. Your library will be the best place for you to start your search. Rich Dad – Poor Dad by Robert Kiyosaki was the first book on real estate investing we ever read. Its premise is simple. Invest for assets that produce cash-flow. Minimize the noise from anything and everything else.

Kiyosaki operates an informative website, YouTube channel and seminars held around the World. While his message contains some questionable content and while he may have had some financial setbacks over the years – the base root of his message remains in-tact and required reading.

Popular TV personalities seen on HGTV and DIY-TV also offer seminars and training classes. These shows air in pretty much any and every market no matter the country or language. They are wonderful entertainment and always show incredible property transformations. Much of the show's content is very carefully staged and always results in the most incredible "reveals" at the end of the show. Take everything with a grain of salt and look for the hidden messages or for ideas rather than turn-key strategies to riches.

My wife and I call these shows "property porn" because it all looks so wonderful when the truth isn't always so certain. We especially have a good laugh when we listen to American shows with the renovation budgets and prices for raw materials and look at our market up here and can't ever seem to find ways bridge the divide. The math doesn't always work so… perfectly.

Attending classes where these "flip" or BRRR strategies (defined shortly) are promoted, all sound wonderful. Audiences must take care to consider the source material for the presentation and whether or not the data being shared is appropriate for your region. Better education might be available through local sources and experts. Do your homework before you commit to any strategy, no matter how good-looking the "porn". We'll take a closer look, a little later on in the book.

To start – you might have cash or liquid investments that you can sell in order to create the required down payment. You might be able to free up an investment capital account, using the equity in your home by establishing a Home Equity Line of Credit, which is what we did to get started. Or you might borrow the down payment(s) from a more established friend or family member.

There are other ways to raise cash via joint partnerships but they are more complex and beyond the simple agenda we are addressing here, at least for now. Your own Catch Up

Investing strategy should take some work but not be overly complicated and scare you from taking action.

Here is the bottom line. By investing in a rental income property – you control an asset that generates cash every month your property is occupied with a tenant, or "client" that helps you pay the bills. In time – depending on the number of units or properties controlled – you have effectively constructed your own personal pension plan and you've done this principally with someone else's money.

The Bottom Line:

1. There are wonderful resources available so you can learn

2. Be wary of paying fees and memberships to clubs and coaches unless and until you do your homework, first. Ask for referrals

3. Seek like-minded individuals who may help shorten your learning curve.

4. Beware the pitfalls of falling for the quick easy solution and false economies of property porn on TV and the Internet.

CHAPTER 8

Who else should be on your team?

Before we start – you might like to flip back to Chapter Two when we introduced the concept of forming your own Personal Board of Directors. The roles and the people who fill them in this chapter would be worthy additions. We failed to include them up until now because we have been dealing with higher level concepts and now need to discuss specifics – especially as your next tasks relate specifically to real estate investing.

Bank Manager

While you may not end up financing your properties via your personal bank, trust or credit union (for reasons we'll get to shortly), your Catch Up Investing adventure likely starts here. That's because unless you have a ready source of cash available to invest today, you may need to rely on using the embedded equity you have locked in your home. Your bank manager or other similar contact will help you set up a Home

Equity Line of Credit (HELOC), giving you the facility to fund down payments on as many properties as you can finance comfortably.

My father once told me that I should always meet and get to know the manager at our bank. I've made it a point to make this all-important connection going all the way back to 1984 when I first graduated from university. Why? The reason is quite simple. In all those years and through all those relationships – our bank manager has become our initial ally and advisor.

We've been approved for mortgages, lines of credit and received very prompt attention when things have gone wrong. Over the years – we have seen greater centralization of authority so today our manager cannot make the magic happen quite the same way but we still benefit from having an inside edge to help us understand our options. Having a key cheerleader and coach at the bank has always paid off for us and likely always will at least to some extent.

Mortgage Broker

Before you start looking at properties – you need to interview and select a mortgage broker. Like us – you may think "I have a great relationship with my bank – why wouldn't I just work with them?" Well it depends on what your goals are and how much financing you'll need to make those goals a reality.

Hitting the rewind button for a moment; please understand that while our journey started with our bank manager in order to establish a HELOC to provide seed capital – we could just have easily started with our mortgage broker.

Mortgage brokers can establish the same facility – perhaps with some revolving credit options that might not be offered by your own bank. Having to do it all over again – I think we still may have gone to our bank as we enjoy a very strong and supportive relationship to this day. But your situation may be different and in the spirit of sharing, wanted to mention that.

We learned that most banks are only comfortable financing a certain number of properties and then you are basically cut off unless your financial circumstances change. By that I mean not only the amount of cash you have but also your ability to cover those mortgages in case your incoming rental income stream is somehow compromised. A licensed mortgage broker will be able to help you come up with a plan to finance the number of properties you wish to purchase – given your financial realities and time horizons.

They do this by developing a hierarchy of lending institutions where they may go to 1 or 2 Schedule A banks (not your own) to fund the purchase of your first 2-5 properties before ever going to *your* bank. Once you've bought as many as you can finance this way and still seek more – they can access other more creative forms of funding including private lenders, albeit at higher cost.

Make sure you recruit a mortgage broker who specializes in funding investment real estate in rental properties. Should you graduate to more esoteric deals such as commercial and mixed use structures – your mortgage broker should reflect these interests and have experience in those markets to help you transact the deal. A mortgage professional that has only funded the purchase of principal homes is not adequately trained and capable of helping you build your investing empire – no matter the size.

Logically this makes sense as you would never go to a general practitioner to do more complex cardio-thoracic or neurosurgery – no matter the similar "Dr." title at the front of their surnames. Ask questions and find out the extent of their experience supporting investors like you.

The most important thing to keep in mind is the limit to which you want to leverage your future. It's all well and good to take advantage of "other people's money" as we discussed earlier; it is another thing entirely to become sucked into the notion you can build the next great real estate empire and end up taking on too much debt in the process of chasing that grandiose dream.

In our case – we determined (in the end) that holding 3 and perhaps 4 properties would create the income we needed - that when added to all of our retirement income sources would generate the standard of living we desired. By the time we will have both stopped working full time – we will have paid down our mortgages and enjoyed property price appreciation to the point where we expect to control 75% - 80% equity in our properties. At this point – we could refinance and invest the sums into other income producing vehicles or restructure our mortgages to minimize mortgage pay-down and maximize the difference between rent collected and mortgage payments owed and perhaps consider different tax management strategies. We might even sell one of our properties or limited partnerships to pay off the remaining balance on our best assets.

Please remember - for us – the idea of making income properties a key part of our retirement plan was to create a personal pension alternative. Our target income for this portion of our living income was to produce between 25% - 30% of our total target income. We had no over-inflated, lofty goals and aspirations of becoming Canada's next real estate tycoons – we just wanted enough to be comfortable.

Realtors

There are two kinds of realtors, well OK – there are likely more but for the purposes of our Catch Up Investing journey – let's *again* say there are only two. The first is well-known to you and probably helped you either buy or sell the home you currently own or plan to own. This would be your principal residence and to date, perhaps the largest purchase you have ever made. The second is more important to you going forward and that is a real estate professional who is experienced in the property rental market.

If you are going to get involved in this market, it makes sense to work with someone who holds their own investment real estate and helped other investors build their financial futures using the asset class. The skills could not be more different. A sales rep who has never had "skin in the game" may be a fair negotiator but will never truly be able to advise you.

A personal real estate agent (if you'll allow me to use that phrase to help identify the players) will help you buy and or sell a home given your personal needs and desires. An investment real estate professional will look at the property through the eyes of an investor and help you avoid the money-traps you might not see.

They will also help you focus, not so much on what would be appealing to you as the principal resident – but your tenant (or client) would want and need and select your best property "bet" over the cute duplex two streets over. You must think of your property as a product and not simply a house. You need to market it and the terms of your lease vs the competition. A realtor who is also a more experienced investor is someone whose advice you need to heed.

How do you find these investment experts?

Recall earlier that we discussed the need for you to take courses, join networks and find like-minded people. They will help you. The Real Estate Investment Network (REIN) organization and Canadian Real Estate Wealth Magazine regularly feature stories from investors and investment-oriented real estate professionals as to how they built their portfolios of properties and helped their clients do the same. Reach out and start interviewing them for a possible seat on your personal board of directors. It's too important a position to simply leave to chance.

Property Managers:

One of the first decisions you will have to make about your rental properties is how hands-on you will be in managing those properties. There are arguments to make for and against and the answer is entirely personal and subjective.

Here are a number of things to consider.

- Do you have the time and temperament to find and manage tenant clients?

- Are you willing to learn how to act as your own property manager and take on the task of either maintaining or arranging regular property maintenance and repairs?

- Are you familiar with rental contract dispute resolution practices, matters of discipline and eviction? Are you willing to learn and perhaps make mistakes until you've mastered the subject matter?

- Are you able and willing to keep yourself current on all related matters to owning and managing your properties?

- Do you have the time to collect rent payments and chase them down when late?

- Do you really want to take phone calls from your tenant clients when something goes wrong – at any and all hours of the day?

We answered "No" to every question, which is why we sought out the services of a reliable property manager. We have professional managers on every property we own. In each case, the managers were recommended by our realtor "coach" as being people known to them and experienced.

In Alberta and as is the case with every other professional relationship we maintain, our property managers are also real estate investors. Lisa and Sid (not their real names, but close enough) are also investors and more experienced than us, owning several doors in addition to the nearly 100 doors they currently manage. Amazingly – they are also quite a bit younger than us which gives us a great deal of comfort in knowing that they are likely to stay with us for as many years as we need.

Lisa is our principal contact as she runs the office and maintains first line of contact with our tenant clients. Sid runs things in the field and effects most onsite repairs and inspections. Because of their hands-on experience (and because we have been lucky enough to forge a close personal relationship) we have come to trust their guidance and follow their advice.

Property managers don't personally benefit when they call you with news of some required repair or client issue. They are looking out for your best interests and want to resolve matters as quickly, appropriately and efficiently as possible. What does that mean to you? Peace of mind. How can you help them? Ask questions and then make a quick decision so they can get on with their business and yours.

If you are lucky enough to find managers as professional and honourable as ours – you must get to a place of trust as quickly as possible. Whenever Sid calls and informs me of something that needs attention – I usually ask what the matter is – their recommendation(s) – and any available options. I then usually follow their guidance to the letter. In the end – you really don't have too many choices; especially when the repair or matter requiring attention deals with basic utilities, appliances or matters dealing with personal safety.

Of course, good property managers do not work for free. We have two principal relationships – although each manages several properties. Lisa and Sid manage individual doors where our other managers manage units in multi-tenant structures. The fees we pay to each manager are quite different. You can expect to pay anywhere from 4.0% to as much as 10.0% of your monthly rent cheques, per door (or controlled house, suite etc.) to your property manager.

You will have to decide if this fee makes sense. Are you confident that your manager has your back? Do they explain things and respond as quickly as you need? Do they handle urgent matters as well and with as much professionalism as they do routine tasks?

In our case – we are very happy to share that professional property management has been an excellent experience. They are worth every penny. They provide us the peace of mind I mentioned earlier; especially given the fact our properties are all located thousands of kilometers away.

We chose to invest in Alberta, Canada because we liked the market and the absence of rent controls. This very fact makes the need for trustworthy property manager partners essential.

The Bottom Line:

1. Your real estate investing success depends on the people whose help you seek. Namely, these people will include your bank manager, mortgage broker and realtor. Don't work with just anyone. You will always be best served by experts familiar and experienced with investing vs. those who will try to sell you a house.

2. Furthermore, unless you have the time, inclination and the interest to fix toilets, find and deal with tenant issues, you may be better off by finding a professional property manager. Again – be sure to hire someone at an acceptable

cost and preferably one who is also an experienced investor. Wouldn't it make more sense to work with someone who's walked in your shoes?

CHAPTER 9

Alternative Real Estate Investment Strategies

Partnering with Builders and Developers

The next few chapters will dig still deeper into your real estate investing options. We'll look at a couple of private equity products we used to generate capital gains vs. income and then close the real estate section by considering some additional, alternative ideas.

The first real estate private equity product we considered on our journey to rebuild our financial wealth was a condo construction finance deal. It is this next strategy we mentioned back at the beginning of Chapter 7.

This program in effect made us partners with leading property developers and their Exempt Market Dealer (EMD) in the Greater Toronto Area (GTA). The premise behind these products is quite simple; residential subdivisions, condo towers and mixed-use projects are designed, built and sold much the same way as any other product, big or small. Manufacturers of consumer products build in a profit margin and so do property developers. It just made sense and we wanted to take part.

Property developers often find it more financially attractive to seek investment partners to advance the funds to secure appealing land for development. Developers enjoy the same benefits of leverage as we do. They commit 20% from their cash reserves (like a down payment) and raise the remaining 80% from individual investors to close the deal. In this case – individual investors act much like the bank – but with one key difference. The entire deal is funded with cash and avoids unnecessary leverage risk.

Sites are chosen to match the right product (houses vs. condo towers etc.) with the right parcel of land, depending on regulatory requirements and the character of the surrounding neighborhood. Very detailed work is completed to service the land and be sure the project is onside with all zoning rules to ensure the land purchase and construction moves forward. The project is designed and priced and then marketed to investors.

Pricing of these deals is one part art and one part science. The price per square foot of each offering must make sense in the context of the surrounding market. Market conditions and the value of real estate and similar projects nearby will define a competitive offering. Priced right – these private equities should return approximately 20% in annualized returns. Of course – projected returns vary and nothing is guaranteed.

The structure of a construction private equity deal may take the form of a mutual fund trust or a limited partnership. We found this appealing, which is why we chose it as our first real estate investment and are still "fans" of the structure. Today, we fund these deals from cash in our registered accounts as we have already taken on enough risk considering the individual properties we now hold. We have always wanted to avoid being over-leveraged.

Our risk exposure in these structures is limited to the amount we invest and nothing more. We also like the chance of being a part of something far greater in size than anything we could afford on our own and a project that comes with a projected exit date.

Once the land purchase closes, a selling centre is opened and then the project is promoted to the public. You've likely seen several of these campaigns in newspapers, on billboards and online. The project is then managed through the selling period, construction phase and closing/exit process.

Once the project sells 70% of all units in the pre-construction selling period – the project would then be eligible for construction financing and actual building. The remaining 30% unsold inventory is released for sale gradually over time at hopefully sequentially higher prices as the project proves its market appeal.

The difference in selling price is realized as time elapses and can be attributed to a rise in the value of the underlying land for the specific project and surrounding real estate (of existing homes and also other new construction projects nearby and under construction). "Hot" projects might sell out when first offered but that should not be considered the norm. Developers will always seek to maximize their profit margin whenever and however they possibly can. The process is simple in design but quite challenging in execution.

Once construction financing has been secured – it is often common for the project to issue a full or partial repayment of your invested capital. Investors then wait for their "profits" until the project is complete – with all residents in possession of their units and accounts settled. Deal structures may vary depending on what is being built and the size and complexity of the project and may range between 2 and 10 years.

So what are the risks?

Projects don't always sell. The economy can turn on you like it did in 2008 when several building projects were placed on indefinite hold. Liquidity is also a concern here; there usually is none. There is more often than not, no regular rent or interest payment from the land under development to help cover your costs. Investors need to be committed to hanging on until the project is complete – which may impact the settlement of estates in the event of death, divorce and bankruptcy of an investor. That's why these deals are usually sold to more sophisticated investors or according to new rules to help smaller investors take part without overcommitting.

This is not buy and hold real estate. You're building a 40 story widget for sale and there's no guarantee it will sell, exit on schedule or sell for the price you expect.

To date – we have exited two deals and continue to hold twelve and will look for more. They have performed exactly as built and projected. We have been very fortunate and are committed to the structure and the partners we selected.

These investments can be held in non-registered or in fully registered accounts such as RRSPs, RRIFs and TFSAs. A minimum investment (usually $25,000) is required for qualified investors. Projects are often over-subscribed and we found we needed to move quickly if interested. Often our requested allotments have been scaled back, similar to initial public stock offerings (IPOs) for the most popular and hot new issues on Bay Street or Wall Street.

While past performance is certainly no guarantee of future results, our private equity construction deals have been an important part of our investment strategy and held primarily in tax-sheltered accounts. We've been fortunate to find the right investment and developer partners who take a disciplined approach to underwriting and risk management.

Thinking of real estate as a product to be manufactured and sold with "built-in" profits and pre-determined exit dates was for us a new way of looking at investing in real estate and we have come to rely on the asset class to help us build our nest egg in ways we had not previously imagined.

US-Based Multi-Tenant

As we continue our look into Real Estate Private Equities, I'd like to share with you our experiences in US multi-tenant projects. Five years ago, we began reading about how the US real estate market in multi-tenant buildings was on fire. The economic recovery had been particularly kind to middle-power US cities such as Phoenix, Dallas and Houston. Patient investors were positioning themselves to reap the benefits.

In particular – there existed a glut of multi-tenant buildings, town home developments and mixed-use structures that were unloved and undervalued. Some of these were sorely in need of upgrade and repair as their owners were still feeling the aftermath of the 2008/09 financial markets crisis and let their buildings fall into disrepair or state of "meh". Some of the strategies employed by opportunistic investors are well-known including "BRRR" (Buy, Renovate, Refinance and Rent: More on that later).

We found that the opportunities for the greatest Net Operating Income (NOI) optimization were situated in US markets where property managers had barely hung on after the financial markets crash. There was an oversupply of properties where current ownership wanted "out" and was willing to accept offers from mostly Canadian investors seeking good returns in a stronger currency. A number of investor syndicates were created using a limited partnership structure where minimum investments of $25,000 secured you a position in the project.

Rent normalization is usually the first task undertaken by new management. This means a 2 bedroom suite should rent for perhaps $1,200 across the board in that townhome complex and not $950, $1,000 and $1,150, which effectively reduces rent disparity and smooth's out expected income.

The next tactic used by these project managers is to evaluate the condition of the units themselves and the buildings common elements, such as pools, gymnasiums, meeting rooms etc. The goal is to complete upgrades and market the building to a higher income demographic. This means upgrading kitchens, bathrooms and adding conveniences such as laundry rooms with washers, dryers and enhanced storage. These simple in-unit upgrades often result in an extra $150 - $200 USD per month, per unit or "door" which significantly adds to the return after costs are covered. These changes can result in NOI growth of up to 60% over a 5-Year period.

As investors, we liked that.

As income increases – so does the value of the building – which may support a possible refinancing of the building. There is of course no guarantee this may be the case as it depends on the investment mandate of the project manager, the "math" on each unit and market conditions. In any event, we determined it was best to take this returned capital and hold it to be deployed into our next deal.

Investing in the US while attractive, presented some additional costs we hadn't fully anticipated. Some of these costs include the need for filing US Federal and State income tax returns. We had no trouble finding accountants who can help cross-border investors and fully recognized that we would have to pay tax on rental income received and capital gains taxes on exit (thankfully mitigated by the taxes withheld) but we weren't prepared for the premium charges for preparing these documents over the costs of similar tax-filer forms in Canada.

Initially – we held the properties in joint form – which requires individual returns for each of my wife and me.

Double the trouble, double the fun! Of course the offsetting tax credits in both countries helps avoid the spectre of double-taxation but our returns were compromised by the several hundreds of dollars each year we had to pay to double file. Today we are investing as a couple in one name only to help avoid these extra costs. We feel safe that should one of us pre-decease the other – we can effectively transfer the property from one name into the other as a tax-free rollover event.

Investing in these packaged deals while convenient, does not absolve you from doing your homework. The offering memorandum documents are usually quite complete and present a great argument for the economic strengths of the market; population dynamics (growth vs. decline), net in-migration and usually a list of the local major employers and their plans for growth. But you need to do your own research to make sure the facts that are shared in any glossy package make sense and can be corroborated.

Still - something could go wrong. In one case – even after having obtaining engineering reports and building inspections; one of our programs required an early exit. In this case, the costs of repairing and renovating the units grew out of line with the deal's initial financial projections. This made the project far less desirable. Fortunately for all – the project manager was able to sell the development to another interested party and we all made money; just not as much as was first anticipated. The end result though was a renewed sense of confidence in our manager. But - I still do my own research.

Target annual returns for this class of product seem to be between 16.0% - 18.0%. Your returns may be higher or lower depending on whether or not you have cash to invest or use leveraged funds from a home equity line of credit (HELOC). Your access to cash and tolerance for risk will determine which way you go. In our situation – we have committed both hard cash dollars and used our HELOC with a very conservative and expedited pay-down schedule. Minimum purchase amounts are usually $25,000 USD and may be subject to allocation if over-subscribed, again like a stock IPO. These deals are only available through EMDs, who will work with investors to ensure suitability.

In our case, we simply wanted access to the multi-tenant structure, in a number of markets without the stress of additional mortgage leverage and risk. We wouldn't be able to hold these assets, have the portfolio of projects and market diversification we have without these products and are committed to staying the course.

What is the last word on this? There are options available with very similar structures right here at home. Good news!

Farmland and True Diversification

 Canadian Eh?

This segment is dedicated to the Canadian market, although similar options may be available elsewhere in the World.

Some time ago, I read a book "The Crash Course" written by Chris Martenson, detailing his views on assets and wealth. He also wrote about the difference between prosperity and growth. The premise is that you cannot have both as growth needs continual expansion which eventually collapses an economy while prosperity occurs when people have enough resources on which to live in comfort, enjoy some of life's finer things and do all this in a broader economy that *is* sustainable.

According to Martenson, a true measure of prosperity is the means by which we actually measure wealth. Martenson theorizes that wealth can be classified as being Primary, Secondary or Tertiary.

Primary wealth exists of the land. Throughout history, the wealthiest family in town owned the most land, farmland, forests, minerals, energy and fisheries. Their wealth existed as those resources were shepherded and sustainably converted to money (gold, silver or other goods by barter) or later into fiat currency, which is what we use as currency today.

Secondary wealth existed as the means by which these land resources are harvested. These included the lumber mills to take the trees and produce lumber or the fruits and crops of the farm land. It stands to reason without primary wealth – those producing the secondary wealth would have no access to or wealth at all.

Finally, Tertiary wealth is paper wealth. It is a claim on wealth and subject to the lowest possible level of control. Stocks and Mutual Funds represent a claim on only the amount of wealth that holders of primary and secondary wealth wish to sell.

Tertiary wealth represents the most fragile wealth as it is so often and easily manipulated.

Canadian farm land might offer the best of both primary and secondary wealth.

Warren Buffett believes that farmland must be bought as an investment based on the yield it produces, just like any other business. The fact that the land itself may fall in value as it did through the early 1980's does not negate the fact that people need to eat and that farmland and the farmers who work it produces food to feed a hungry nation. Since then, savvy and well-known investors have sought out investing in farmland as an asset that is nearly perfectly, negatively correlated to public securities traded in the stock market. It has been equated to gold and other commodities that do well in times of turmoil and also provides a sound hedge against inflation.

Farmland values follow something called an "asymmetric risk curve" which means the land will always have value. The same cannot be said for stocks and some fixed income instruments like corporate bonds (i.e. Nortel, Bre-Ex etc.). This delivers an additional measure of safety in uncertain times.

We recently learned that Michael Bury (of "The Big Short", the analyst who called the last great financial markets crash in 2008) is also a big proponent of farmland having moved into that sector (as well as into Gold) as he exited the stock and financial markets as the crash enveloped North America

There are many ways to play the farmland market. You could purchase the land directly and either "work" the fields or rent them out to farmers who would pay attractive rent. You might consider publically traded REITs that employ the same buy-and-rent strategy, but then you would be subjected to the same public markets idiosyncrasies (that I've mentioned earlier in our journey together) including panic selling and stress brought on by market pundits who do nothing to help long term investors. Or you could seek similar diversified and professionally managed portfolios of farmland properties within private equities from EMDs.

Each of these investment vehicles offer the potential for different types returns. Public REITS may offer more up-front income and capital gains. Private equities often rely on structures that feature return-of-capital provisions as well as conventional income and capital gains. Do your homework as they are all different.

It's up to you. Farmland is promoted online, by realtors (i.e. realtor.ca) and can be financed by banks, private lenders or Farm Credit Canada. Larger down payments are usually required of 30% or better. But investors are flocking to the asset class.

In some Canadian Provinces, there are ownership restrictions. Canadian citizen, non-Saskatchewan residents are limited to the amount of farmland they can hold and foreign investors are precluded entirely from buying SK farmland at all. These restrictions have effectively held back the rise in SK farmland prices per acre. Should these restrictions be lifted, the projections for increases in values are impressive – even beyond what they have been to date.

Consider the recommended long term appreciation levels for residential real estate in Canada (ex. Vancouver and Toronto) of 3% - 4% annually, mentioned earlier in this book. Canadian farmland has appreciated on average 4.92% annually since 1985 and 11.55% since 2009. Saskatchewan farmland has appreciated in value by 4.19% and 13.69% over the same reporting periods. And yet SK farmland is still undervalued when compared to similar adjacent farm lands in Canada and the United States. (data provided by Farm Credit Canada)

Evaluating farmland is by no means easy. Hands-on investors would have to see the land, evaluate the nutrient health of the soil, topography (hills, flatlands, peaks and valleys, which could affect operating costs) proximity to adequate water, available transport, storage and labour. Should you choose to rent the land to farmers, you would need representation to negotiate the best rents and terms to make sure your income was steady and safe. This all might be possible with the right property managers and agents but a fool's errand if tried on your own without specialized knowledge.

Then there is the matter of diversification. Does owning one property constitute appropriate diversification? What crops will your land produce? Into what markets will you sell; domestic or international? Do you have the contacts? Avoiding all these considerations is the unique selling proposition of the packaged investment that can represent several farms with varied crops (commodity and high value, high margin) and sales contracts for the resulting crops and production.

Today, there are 7.7 Billion souls that inhabit the World. In 2050, the United Nations projects that number to reach 9.7 Billion. Today, arable farmland with nutrient-rich soil is being sold to property developers, stressing the remaining acres to produce the food we need to feed the World's hungry masses. When supply is constrained and demand expands, the only outcome can be increases in food prices and values of the land on which it's produced. You might want to think about that when you consider just how truly diversified are your real estate holdings?

Water Wealth

 ## Canadian Eh?

This segment is dedicated to the Canadian market, although similar options may be available elsewhere in the World.

According to corroborating information on www.waterfootprintcalculator.com and www.statista.com, Canadians are among the World's largest users of fresh water each and every year. Use is measured in the production of all goods and services produced and consumed. Americans use 2,200 gallons per person per day, 365 days of the year and we are not far behind, using just under 1,700. Water is an indispensable part of our lives and its judicial management will only become more critical as we move forward.

But how are investors best able to participate in the water market?

You could seek out existing and new companies that develop water infrastructure and purification technologies. As is of then the case – you might select the right industry but choose exactly the wrong individual company, technology and associated stock. Finding an appropriate Exchange Traded Funds (ETFs) would buffer selection risk by buying a basket of such firms.

There are many publically traded ETFs that hold water-related processing and infrastructure development companies. Such information is widely available and readers should be encouraged to speak to their advisors.

As we examined in the last chapter – the development of Canada's farmland is a vital part of the legacy we leave for future generations. The degree to which that legacy depends on us shepherding our vital water resources is something we currently don't fully appreciate.

Some perspective: it takes 674 gallons of water to develop only 6 ounces of steak and nearly as much to process one hamburger patty. Fully 52 gallons of water are used to produce 1 egg (624 per dozen). 22 gallons of water are needed to produce only 1 lb of plastic and yet twice that are required to produce 1 plastic water bottle. Given so much of our national GDP is produced for export markets as well as national consumption – it should be no surprise that we rely so much on this precious resource.

But this section of the book is dedicated to real estate investing which means everything we discuss should relate to the use and development of land, commerce, housing and rental properties.

bar

Municipalities and towns depend on access to fresh water, the treatment and disposal of waste water, lands for the development of roads and a master plan for land use and subdivision. This all must happen before developers are given their mandates and the first shovels break ground.

In Alberta, access to and securing the rights for water must be confirmed and in-hand before the town's development and expansion plans can even be considered – which is where investors may find their opportunity. In 2007 Canada's first market based exchange was created in Alberta to match sellers of water rights with those who require access to further the expansion and development of their towns and farming properties. As in most things, up front capital is required to secure these rights and in 2014 a price was set at $2,500 per acre foot. This price depends on the allocation of water required to support the projects being considered.

Town development requires so many acres of land and hence a proportional amount of water rights per acre foot to service the land's eventual requirements for the people and businesses located on that land. These requirements will support the production and consumption of goods and services in that town. Recall the point we made earlier where the average uses of water by Canadians equals some 1,700 gallons per person per day and you can soon see why this is such an important key in a town's future.

Town planners and developers need access to capital to secure these rights – which is where investors come in to play a role.

Each project must stand on its own merits and is not guaranteed. Intermediaries are appointed to seek and obtain approvals for each project. The good news for investors is however, that eventually – water rights are secured and approved projects are moved forward to when water rights will be required. At this point, an Exempt Market Dealer (EMD) gets involved to find capital from investors who will seek to fund the purchase of water rights by developers with those seeking to sell.

Usually – these projects are funded and exited in between 3 – 5 years. Minimum investment amounts for investors who qualify under the exempt rules are quite modest at $5,500 in TFSA accounts and $10,000 in other registered and non-registered accounts. Returns may include annual income flow of between 8.0% - 10.0% and performance bonuses at the project's completion. Performance bonuses are determined by the eventual sales price of the unserviced land (you still need infrastructure, gas, power etc.) and the related price of the water rights at the same time the deal is confirmed. Like many private equity deals – there may be ongoing management fees, acquisition costs and results are not guaranteed.

Again like most private equities – these projects are illiquid – with no guarantee of a secondary market to exit the deal should investors wish or require an early exit. Projects may also face delays which may in turn delay the projected exit date. This means investors should commit only such capital they can afford to risk and hold until the project is complete.

Should the land sell for prices below those projected, returns may not achieve expectations and the share of desired profits over and on top of the income portion of the returns may disappoint. Investors may receive profit participation returns of 3.5% to 16% in addition to any interest income they receive. If the approved development plan is approved where less water is required to support the plan; it may be possible to sell those water rights without additional cost and hence greater profit to the investor syndicate.

Remember that the purest forms of wealth come from primary sources including land, water and the natural resources found therein. As compelling as that may be, every deal is different – so be sure to read the fine print.

The Bottom Line:

1. Housing, like anything else is a product. Units are made, marketed and sold and priced with a manufacturer's markup built into the price paid.

2. The units (houses, town homes, condos and mixed use buildings) are priced in the context of the surrounding properties. Developers will price in profits that should generate annualized returns for investors in excess of 15%-20%.

3. Returns like this can fuel the growth of both non-registered and fully registered accounts.

4. Wealth can be created from the land and water. "They're not making any more if it these days!"

CHAPTER 10

What else can we do?

Full disclosure; I have not personally tried any of the techniques and strategies highlighted in this chapter. I can share with you what I've heard, read and learned and am breaking slightly with the original premise of this book because I believe that these investing strategies may prove to be quite effective for some of you. Each strategy has its own objective, need for cash and time frame. One of the strategies may result in a long term hold position, although each strategy can be employed several times and become a potential long-term method for creating wealth. Your window of opportunity depends on the amount of capital you can raise from your own sources or with the help of others.

Let's begin.

Flips:

Back in Chapter 6, I shared with you my thoughts on HGTV and DIY TV "property porn" shows that make it seem easy for anyone to buy houses cheap – fix them up and sell them for handsome profits. While that may be true in many cities across Canada and the United States, it might not always be possible, in every city.

The cost of housing is very different from city to city as well as is the costs for closing, contractors and raw materials. The cost of shipping heavy items like flooring and granite may make for a bargain in Las Vegas and seem like an insurmountable road block in Vancouver.

The key to making good flips happen profitably is dependent on getting the best deal on a property that is within your abilities to finance the house purchase *and* the renovation. The money is made when you buy – almost as much – if not more than when you sell. So you have to know your market and do the math on every step along the way from purchase through renovation to the final sale.

Obviously there would be additional costs to include. Closing costs, real estate fees and applicable land-transfer costs, utilities costs (during renovation and through the selling period) as well as incidental costs like travel to and from the property and marketing costs that will all eat into the gross profits you hope to make. Attractive top line revenue could get squeezed pretty tight if you don't factor in all these additional costs adequately. The end effect would be anywhere from wonderful to disastrous depending on how accurate is your financial blueprint.

There are plenty of training seminars and online resources to teach you the business. I think you might be better-served by finding a reputable contractor and mentor on resource sites and networking communities like REIN (also previously mentioned) who can share their experiences in a more supportive environment.

Seriously motivated investors may even like to take the extraordinary step of either partnering with an established realtor or taking the courses required to get licensed to sell real estate themselves. The extra 2.5% saved (from split commissions) may add as much as an extra $7,750 on a home worth $310,000 when you buy and an additional $9,125 on the sale of the same home post-renovation – assuming you sell the home at $365,000. The total savings of over $16,000 might help to make the overall project profitable, depending on the amount you invested in renovation costs and the time taken to buy, renovate and sell to exit the project.

Taking our illustration one step further – let's assume you invested $30,000 in renovation costs so your total gross profit is $25,000 plus the $16,000 in real estate fees for a total of $41,000. Let's extend the illustration further to say the project took 90 days from start to finish; meaning you might be able to complete 4 such projects each year. That means you could generate an additional annual income of $164,000. Consult with your account as your tax code may treat this as capital gains – or – as earned income if you are deemed to be in the business of flipping houses.

This is where a conversation with your accountant may be in order to discuss organizing your business activities within an incorporated structure.

While we're exploring the art-of-the-possible – let's say we pay half of the sums mentioned above out each year in income taxes and are left with $82,000 Net. If you could find an investment (we profiled a few earlier) that could generate an 8% annual return – and "run the model" making the exact same after-tax contribution and subject to exactly the same kind of growth over a 10 year period – your total potential portfolio could be enhanced by an additional $1.28 Million.

OK – here comes the caveat. These numbers assume you make exactly $82,000 – four times per year and reinvest every dollar made. It further assumes no increase or decrease in costs or profitability – makes no adjustment for market changes over time – your ability to finance such deals and see them through successfully. It also has not been adjusted for any taxes payable along the way. So yes – this is "pie-in-the-sky" kind of thinking – but I'd be willing to bet that this line of thought would work for at least some of you.

I'd bet further that if some of you are handy and can effect some of the work yourself – that your costs and profitability might be enhanced over and above the math I've shared with you here. This also might just be the perfect side job to do in semi-retirement and so I recommend you use a factor of 50% (which is what I did here) to cover taxation if you want to extend and confirm the illustration and make it more fitting to your personal circumstances.

Flipping houses is not a strategy for the faint of heart as you may uncover surprises you couldn't possibly anticipate when you open up a wall or run into plumbing, electrical and structural challenges you might not see with only a surface-view when buying the house. Be prepared for losses, stress and heart-ache along the way. The rewards however, might just be the ticket to supercharging your Catch Up Investing journey.

Buy-Renovate-Refinance-Rent (BRRR):

Buy-Renovate-Refinance-Rent (or "BRRR" as it is known among investors) is a strategy quite similar to the flipping strategy described above. The difference is that while investors buy-fix and sell or flip properties for capital gains (see note on taxation – income vs. capital gains above) – investors who choose the BRRR methodology are motivated to hold the properties long term and enjoy the cash flow and mortgage pay-down of having a longer horizon time frame in mind. This long term hold approach may also help you avoid the earned income vs. capital gains conundrum.

Investors interested in BRRR would face the same deal metrics of flipping properties. The "money" would be made when the deal is first contemplated. Can you find a bargain? What would be the renovation budget? What renovations could you fund or afford? How much could your renovation enhance the property's value and resulting monthly rent? Would you find a bank, lending institution or partner who could help you finance the deal? Would you have the time and expertise to manage the home as a rental property going forward? (Please see my comments earlier on the value of great property managers).

Investors who seek to make BRRR a systematic strategy would be wise to consider the "Refinance" element of BRRR as they could pull out tax-free dollars and reinvest that capital in the next project. They could of course sit on the capital

---

appreciation or refinance their mortgage to maximize amortization and enhance cash flow each month. They could of course elect to use capital depreciation to further enhance their monthly cash flow. There are myriad strategies and models to follow. Again – do your homework and seek advice.

Rent-to-Own (RTO):

While Flip strategies evolve from purchase to sale over months at a time; Rent-to-own (RTO) strategies occur in the medium-term over periods of 3-4 years. The past 10 years have been challenging for many families living at or barely into what we have been conditioned to call the "Middle Class" in most Western economies. While job numbers have been encouraging – the divide has widened between the top 1% and the rest of us who have found it challenging to make ends meet. That frequently means taking jobs beneath previous earnings and cobbling together careers of part time positions to try and cover the bills.

Many families suffered financial hardships in the last financial crisis and have still yet to fully recover. Young singles and families are finding it nearly impossible to move out of their parent's homes and establish roots of their own. Families working through financial proposals (working their way out of insolvency or bankruptcy) are finding it particularly difficult to buy a home as the goal line continues to move annually, just beyond their reach - especially in our largest cities where property values have soared.

In Canada, there exists the financial stress test where mortgages are approved for home buyers based on interest rates for borrowed funds well-above current rates to be sure they can still afford their homes when rates start to increase. If young singles and families could find the funds for a down payment – they often fail to get approved because they simply don't make enough money to qualify.

The result of all this is that people continue to rent, live at home or move further out from the city to find a more affordable housing option. Economically this may not make sense as costs would continue to spiral for things such as daycare, an additional car and the time associated with longer commutes. If credit rates have been bruised since 2008 – then the task of finding an acceptable and affordable housing option become even more stretched.

RTO strategies have become popular as they were created to bridge the divide between those who have made progress back from the financial abyss and the banks and lending institutions that seem reluctant to support their dreams of home ownership.

The RTO model starts with a family who need to find a home. The family has either suffered a financial hardship like a job loss, illness or divorce that has somehow affected their credit rating. This lower credit rating is usually what stands between them and the approval they need to secure a mortgage.

The strategy matches investors who want to make good returns on their invested capital and are socially motivated to help and "do good" in the World and help this pool of financially stressed buyers with bruised credit. Investors buy the homes and create a forward "Option" (defined in Chapter 5) to sell that home to the potential homeowner at some point down the road. The rental term is usually between 3-4 years – which allows the buyer the chance to build-up their credit rating by meeting their monthly rent obligations on time over the rental period so they can eventually purchase the home at a pre-arranged price.

These RTO funding structures are very common elsewhere, funding home appliances, furnaces, water heaters, TVs and furniture. Here is how they work. For our purposes – we'll assume everything happens concurrently (at the same time).

- Prospective homeowner wants to buy a house and may have some amount of down payment.

- Prospective homeowner has a bruised credit rating and while they may make enough money to carry a mortgage – do not have a solid credit rating required to secure bank approval.

- Investor buys the house and structures a contract where they will rent or lease the home to the buyer for a period of between 3-4 years and sell that home at the end of the lease period. This arrangement is defined in what can be described as an "option to purchase" on the part of the homebuyer. The option period may be extended or expire worthless if something goes wrong.

- The lease can either be fixed for the period or stepped with regular increases reflecting what would have been paid in a standard rental contract.

- A portion is either added or allocated from the rent – which is usually higher than market rents in the area. This added or allocated portion is held in an account that is applied to the purchase of the house when the purchase option is exercised.

- The prospective buyer also comes up with a down payment that is also applied to the future purchase price of the house.

- The home is rented for the lease term and rent is paid and collected on time. Regular payment performance is recorded and a statement is provided by the investor to help the purchaser qualify for a conventional mortgage at the end of the term.

There are a number of variations on this model. The most important is the philosophy behind the matching of purchaser and investor.

There are a number of services that coach investors into buying a home and then finding the best possible RTO candidates to take on the RTO mandate. In some situations, renovations may be required in order to make the home presentable. While this order of find-rent-sell works well – it does put all the pressure on the investor to find-fund and then find an interested buyer; which as you know carries risk including costs and timing that may or may not be feasible.

There is another approach that reaches out to find those same prospective homeowners in advance and then takes steps to find an investor who can help them purchase their dream home even if the future owner has bruised credit. All the investor needs to do is be the stake-horse purchaser that allows the entire transaction to evolve end-to-end over a reasonable time horizon, benefiting all stakeholders along the way.

The benefits of this owner-first approach are quite simple.

For an investor, it makes the most critical parts of the deal a reality; namely finding the right buyer who has already taken the trouble of finding a home they love and want to make their own. The risk of finding the house and then hoping they can find the right buyer, who hopefully feels some kind of attachment and desire for that house, can best be described as putting the proverbial cart before the horse.

In general – both models benefit the investor as the buyer takes on all responsibility to maintain the house. This includes funding their own repairs, painting walls and maintaining yards. This will be at some known point in the future become someone's dream, "forever home" as tenant transitions to home owner.

While most conventional rental contracts stipulate tenants need to cut the grass and shovel the walkways and driveways – pretty much everything else remains a cost to the investor aka landlord. But RTO deals are structured to maximize cash flow which is music to an investor's ears.

So what are the down sides to RTO investing?

In actual fact – there don't appear to be many. These are the ones that occurred to me as I sat to write this portion of the book.

- RTO deals have a finite lifespan. That means you will need to find additional deals with hopefully similar or better opportunities as you exit from each contract. No one can say for sure what those opportunities may be in the future.

- Finding the future deals will likely come with higher initial purchase prices – which creates additional stress for investors as the market may move beyond their capacity to fund down payments and finance the purchase themselves.

- Clients may default on their Option Agreements. There may be both good and bad in this depending on the social contract you have with the buyer. Do you keep the down payment? Do you help them out by refunding all or a portion? Do you extend the term? These matters may create a moral dilemma that would not exist in a standard purchase and rent deal structure.

- Finally – there may be a time lag between the time you exit one deal and get into another. The act of "flipping" RTO deals also comes with additional closing and real estate fees that a buy-and-hold strategy avoids. These realities need to be factored into your decision-making process.

There is however an additional benefit to taking advantage of the RTO mandate and that is time and term certainty.

If a 50 year old investor has the funds and earnings to qualify to finance the purchase of 5 units at any one time – then they theoretically have enough time to fund and exit between 20 – 25 deals in total throughout their investment time horizon (say 10 years) assuming everything works like clock-work and they exit each deal on schedule.

The opportunities for cash-flow are remarkable and often better than long-term buy-hold and rent. Because the deals are constructed to maximize monthly cash-flow – they may also be suitable for investors in their retirement years – providing they qualify for the underlying mortgage.

The opportunities for capital gains are also more finite as they are defined in each contract – usually with between 3% - 5% annual price increases. The exit from each contract would however trigger a disposition and taxable event on each transaction. But this too isn't all bad as your rent and capital gains to be paid while you are still working. This may effectively handle the need for a more elaborate tax-management plan (like a life insurance policy) when you eventually collapse your plan and turn all that cash into some other income producing vehicle like a public or private REIT or other private equity, income producing investment.

RTO deals are also possible – perhaps more close to home. Available coaching firms specialize in helping match investors and buyers or teach investors to find their own buyers. Having to do it all over again – I know which path I would have taken and can assure you RTO would have been a central theme in our own Catch Up Investing plan.

Joint Venture Partnerships:

At some point, you're going to run out of money. If that's not the case – then why the Hell did you buy this book?

The fact is that most banks and lending institutions will only lend you so much money. Our mortgage broker said that it was usual that after having financed 5 properties – your principal bank will seek to shut you down. This is why it is so important to work with a mortgage professional – who will seek to find a principal lender – other than your own bank to finance your first 5 properties and then go to another prime lender – then perhaps another before going to your own. The path would then lead to Schedule 2 or B banks, trust companies and private lenders, assuming of course you continually raise the funds needed for the conventional 20% down payments you need to continue buying properties.

Believing that most of you out there will be using your home equity lines of credit to fund these purchases (as we did) the likelihood is that you will run out of funds and may not be able to take on more risk; even if you wanted. If you are in any way motivated to continuing building-out of your real estate empire (beyond us) – you will have to bring on partners with money to help fund your goals.

Attracting Joint Venture or JV partners is a unique skill as the value proposition is often hard to explain. What you are seeking to do is find someone who will advance the down payment funds – which are not insignificant – and agree to share with you an equal portion of the final equity, built up in the property. So the question is; why would someone do that?

They must completely value the expertise you bring to the table. The next question might be – where would you find such individuals?

I would imagine you would find them anywhere you find and meet people who have similar goals as you, the means to support the objective and for whatever reason the lack of time or motivation to learn the process themselves. These people could be friends, co-workers (perhaps dicey), family members and their extended contacts. As I said – my wife and I haven't yet gone down this path so I can only imagine (after having read up on "JV's") the following:

- Financially – these deals need to make sense. I rather doubt that anyone would put upwards of $60,000 - $100,000 down and simply give up 50% of the value of the JV partnership – even if you do all the work.

- You might suggest an income split where the partner receives up to 100% of the net rent, free cash flow until their down payment has been recouped and then everything is split 50/50.

- Before that sum is reached – you will have enter into an Agreement that decides who pays what portion of any required additional costs – i.e. that may not be covered by rent collected – i.e. repairs or large-scale required maintenance for roofing, appliances etc.

- You will have to develop a very complete sales story of the work you will do to earn your keep. This will include the relationships you bring to the table in real estate specialists to help find the right property as well as property managers to help find the best tenants and help you maintain the dwelling.

- The main task for you is finding the right JV partners. Preferably – you'll find them among or related to people you already know. The alternative is to work with strangers. Either way – you will be entering into a long term relationship with these people. Friends may become estranged and strangers may become – well, more strange. The question you need to ask yourself is – "do I want that kind of stress in my life?" The answer for us has been up until now been – No – but you might be open to the idea.

 Canadian Eh?

Some of the ideas in this chapter are not uniquely Canadian but I can offer you some uniquely Canadian partners and resources to help make your RTO and JV strategies a reality. Please reach out to me if you would like to learn more. www.Catch Up Investing.ca

The Bottom Line:

1. Flips, BRRR, Rent-to-Own and JV strategies are all proven real estate investment strategies that can either supplement or supplant a traditional real estate investment plan.

2. Each of these ideas can generate superior cash flow.

3. Each of these ideas require a level of participation if not outright attention compared to a traditional buy-hold-rent traditional model.

4. Some of these strategies may be decidedly more short-term and may also attract additional tax consequences.

CHAPTER 11

Flow Through Shares

 Canadian Eh?

With apologies to my American, British and Australian friends as well as to anyone else living abroad; this entire chapter is another one dedicated entirely to Canadian investors as this product was designed to benefit only those who reside in this country.

Canadians are World-renown hewers of wood and drawers of water. To that, you might add miners of minerals, drillers of oil and gas and refiners of all things resource-based. To that end – Canadian tax code supports the exploration for and development of those natural resources as we harvest and sell them around the World - and utilize them right here at home.

This support has existed for decades in Canadian tax code in both the Canadian Exploration Expense Credit (CEE) and the Canadian Mineral Exploration Tax Credit (CMET). These tax credits allow for an up to 100% tax credit (CEE) and an additional 15% tax credit (CMET) against any source of Canadian generated income (interest, dividends, earned income or capital gains). In some cases – the credits must be applied over a two-year period but none-the-less provide for 100% tax relief.

Recall in Chapter Ten, Chris Martensen's definition of Primary Wealth being resources of the Earth itself that can be extracted, developed and sold. That pretty much describes the backbone of the Canadian economy. As such – it has always been in Canada's best interest to support the exploration for and development of our resources be they oil and gas, minerals or anything else.

Funds raised through initial offerings are allocated into a blind pool that is invested into publically traded shares of small company or "cap" stocks and several private equities that are not yet available on any stock exchange. A "blind pool" is "blind" because the investor has no say in the securities selected by the issuer and if there are several issues each year – each pool may be quite different. The investor would have no knowledge of which pool into which they invested. The funds are allocated by each of the subject firms into their exploration budgets and activities for the year ahead and the chips will fall where they may.

The funds are usually held for a 2-year lock up period. At the end of the second year – the investor will have had the benefit of their allowable tax deductions and the companies would have either been successful in their search, have failed miserably or realized a result somewhere in between. An evaluation is made at that point of the total value of all securities in the pool and the pool is then wound-up by transferring it into a liquid trading vehicle – which is more often than not a closed mutual fund.

Because investors have enjoyed their tax deduction benefits – each fund is treated as a separate issue and not usually made available to new investors. Within the fund, the companies still standing will continue their operations and investors will enjoy in the upside of their continuing operations. This means that they would be entitled to their proportionate share of any resulting dividends and special cash disbursements the companies and the fund in total, produce. This is usually the express maturity option for the funds going forward; to produce an ongoing dividend income stream for investors – usually targeted between 6% - 8% annually – paid either quarterly or monthly. This is a pretty attractive target yield especially in today's low interest environment.

But what if the investor doesn't want the ongoing income? Believe it or not – there may indeed be a good reason that we'll cover in a few minutes. The investor simply may want to sell their fund and look for their next big thing.

In this case the sale would trigger a capital gain of 100% of the remaining value of the fund. Why? Because you received a 100% tax deduction for the entire value of your investment and in the case of an investment entirely dedicated to the mining sector – you may have enjoyed an additional 15% tax deduction. Canada Revenue Agency frowns on the nature of double-dipping – hence the 100% capital gain tax burden on the sale of your funds 2 years down the road.

But is this necessarily all bad news? No.

Remember what our mission is. We are looking to help Canadians who have suffered financial set back including business losses and financial setbacks where they may have capital losses they've carried forward on their income tax profiles for many years. If you have such a capital loss and have invested a sum into a "flow through" – taken your 100% tax deduction and then decide to sell – then you will trigger a capital gain as soon as the sale is made. You would simply offset the capital gain from the sale against that old capital loss carried forward. Everything washes out and you can repeat the process until your entire capital loss has been negated back to ground zero.

In fact the process can be repeated even if you don't have capital losses. You could simply sell – pay tax – reinvest – get a new tax deduction – shelter the tax paid with the new deduction – rinse and repeat.

Perhaps some numbers would help:

First let's assume for this illustration, your blind pool neither makes – nor loses money over its 2-Year term. Let's further assume the investor's marginal tax bracket is 43.7%.

If our investor is an employee and holds the security personally – they will get back $4,370 on an initial $10,000 investment. Pretty simple math so far, right?

In 2 years – the fund matures and rolls-over into a mutual fund with the same $10,000 value. Remember one of our assumptions listed above.

If the investor holds the funds – they can simply hold without triggering any tax – except for the annual taxes owed on any income and dividends produced by the underlying mutual fund they now hold. If the investor decides to sell – they trigger a capital gain on the entire amount. Here's where it gets interesting.

Capital gains receive very favorable tax treatment as only half the gain is taxed.

In our example – this means 50% of the $10,000 value – or $5,000 is taxed. The marginal tax rate is still 43.7% - which derives taxes owed of $5,000 x's 43.7% or $2,185.

In total – this is where the investor stands.

Invested Total	$10,000
Tax deduction produces return of	4,370
Total at Risk	5,630
Value at rollover maturity and sale	10,000
Capital Gains Taxes Owed	2,185
Net Total	7,815

Return on at Risk Equity ($7,815/$5,630) 138.8%* in 2 Years

Now THAT'S what I call "Catch Up Investing"!

Note*: Okay – here comes the fine print. The resulting value of the resulting underlying mutual fund seldom exactly equals the value of your initial investment. The value may be higher – it may be lower. The difference on either side may be slight or it might be great. Remember – these are small cap companies which are inherently of higher risk and the timing of the flow through offering in terms of where resources are in the economic cycle will play a huge role in the value of your returns. Some years you will win big – some – not so much and others you will lose big. The idea is to keep a longer term perspective.

Please Note: There are some new "flow through" products that do not roll over into an income producing fund. These vehicles are built with a mandate to exit and trigger a disposition of the asset and hence a taxable event. Recall your options.

Even with the down side of fund loss and capital gains explained; these vehicles are very much worth considering.

I recall a high-wage, business owner client I had many years ago who had a $100,000 Capital loss on his books because of a bad investment. He came to me asking if there was any way to negate that loss. I explained the entire scenario of how flow through shares worked and the risks associated with making an investment. I also explained to him it might not be possible to completely clear the loss in one simple transaction.

Well in his case – he won the proverbial trifecta.

It was the early 2000's and oil was at a historically low price per barrel of crude. Flow through share issuers had a field day picking up bargains and the resulting rollover mutual funds values enjoyed stellar returns as the price of crude rebounded.

My high-wage earning client enjoyed the immediate tax relief from the 100% tax deduction he accessed (90% in the first year and 10% in the second). The underlying securities all went up in value so the fund was in a gain position at the rollover event. His $100,000 had in fact grown to over $150,000. He sold the fund – applied his $100,000 tax loss carried-forward and paid capital gains tax on the residual $50,000.

Needless to say – he was pretty happy camper.

But this story is not normal nor should you come to rely on it as the absolute certain experience that you might achieve today.

Speaking of "today"; what is the current climate for flow through investing?

Well, it's like this; flow through investing ain't what it used to be.

We have all heard how the oil and gas market in Alberta and Saskatchewan has been hard hit. Our energy resources are land-locked without an easy channel to markets in Eastern Canada, Europe or Asia from the Canadian West. That leaves us with only one market and that's the United States.

Because we have been forced into a position as a price-taker by our sole monopoly buyer – our Western Canadian Select and Liquid Natural Gas products are sold at huge discounts to World prices. There seems to be no support in Ottawa to find a solution to the problem as Federal and provincial governments on both sides of the country impose export hurdles like the tanker moratorium and lack of easement and right-of-way access for pipelines. This means the land-locked reality of our energy markets is not likely to change anytime soon.

This means there has been a loss of appetite to bring oil and gas flow through shares to market for several years. There are however, still offerings for mineral exploration flow through products that are structured identically and provide the same kinds of return potential. And who knows – maybe our lack of support for Canadian energy will be corrected one day under more supportive and fair regimes in Ottawa, Victoria and Quebec City and we will see a return to an interest in this strategy.

As you can tell – I am a believer and supporter of the Canadian energy industry and although I do not live in the West – have very strong family, friend and business ties to the West and respect completely their markets, social construct and fierce need for a fair deal… but that's another book and I have yet to finish this one.

To those of you who feel resource extraction of any kind is somehow bad or unsustainable and at odds with the environment – I would invite you to actually do the research into Canadian environmental standards and the condition of lands post-extraction as compared to the post-extraction condition of lithium mines and resource extraction and environmental records of regimes elsewhere in the World, including those in the Middle East and Africa. But again, I digress.

Assuming my political rant hasn't dissuaded you from considering an investment in flow through shares – you may have some additional questions.

Where can I buy flow through shares?

Flow through shares are offered direct by issuers, through Exempt Market Dealers (EMDs) and Fully licensed securities firms (not financial planners, insurance professionals or mutual funds dealers unless they are also securities licensed).

Are all flow through shares created equal?

No. As in most cases, issuer excellence and track record – while not guaranteed are an indication of their performance in the past. If an issuer has a track record of beating their peers it is more likely they will continue to perform in the future, unless of course there is a material change in managers or the sector falls completely out of favor. (Opinion)

How much money should I invest and how often?

While the business case could be made for flow through investing and the match seems very compelling – investors need to recognize that these investments are perhaps the most speculative of any I've profiled so far in the book. I have used these vehicles in my professional past and for my family – so I am comfortable taking that risk. That doesn't means they are exactly right for you.

Because the purchase price is so reasonable – you might consider investing $10,000 each year into a new series; provided you can find an issuer that gives you confidence and you have the earnings to support taking such risk. You might be in a position to commit more funds in time – especially if you make good money today where you might not have in the past, can accept the risk and perhaps have capital losses on your books to be negated.

A regular amount invested will let you create a ladder of sorts of the different markets in which the resource economy exists. If the economy is hot one year – then values may be good but the choice of securities may be more constrained. If the market has been more challenged and even beaten up and the products are still being offered (by no means certain) then issuers would enjoy their pick of the litter so to speak and you might get great companies at bargain prices. This would be quite beneficial at rollover time where the fund might have enjoyed bounce-back pricing and drive higher values.

The story here is no different than the one you've probably heard all your life about dollar-cost-averaging. Buy some high, buy some low, buy some in the middle. Your average pricing will net-out to your benefit over time. Patience and a long term horizon is key. You would be best to consider a flow through strategy over a 10 year period and avoid cherry picking the market. As in most cases – you will be better-off being approximately right vs. precisely wrong.

CHAPTER 12

Low Hanging Fruit:

We're coming to the end of our Catch Up Investing journey together and yet there are a number of additional items to share. Think of this chapter as a lightening round of sorts where I'll cover some simple ideas and introduce a few more where you may have some homework to do. Here goes.

Executive Compensation:

OK – let's start with the most complex item we'll cover – if for no other reason we can make you aware of the opportunity and invite you to consult with the accounting, legal and insurance members of your personal board of directors and seek additional guidance. You will need help here!

This section will be of particular interest to small business owners and self-incorporated professionals (which now includes Real Estate Reps in Ontario who are not "Brokers" and the heads of Real Estate practices). Executive compensation options include Individual Pension Plans, Personal Pension Plans and Retirement Compensation Agreements. These retirement options were created for owners of small businesses and senior or executive employees who might also be owners or part owners of their firms.

The notion here provides companies and their key personnel with vehicles to fund retirement options equivalent to defined benefit pension plans when those options might not be available to them or might not have been set up in the past. The secret is the amount of money that can be contributed as past service in lieu of RRSP payments, skipped or other retirement accounts that would not provide the same level of contribution room.

There may also be additional legacy options for the transfer of wealth between generations in a family business and facilities to provide enhanced retirement options for business owners to withdraw cash from their companies before selling that are in excess of any available lifetime capital gains exemption rules.

These plans are quite complex, come with a variety of different elements, options and obligations in terms of annual funding and reporting requirements. These will carry additional costs and should only be set up by "companies" with the cash flow and stability to maintain them. They truly are meant for incorporated entities and as such are not meant for everyone reading this book. But for those of you who are business owners or executive connected persons and or employees – they could be the secret to making up for lost time, while you were so busy building up your businesses.

Don't do this one yourself at home!

Side Hustle:

One of the things that occurred to me a couple of years ago is this; I watch way too much damn TV. At the end of the day – I used to crash on the couch, turn on the tube and watch or stream whatever idiotic show looked interesting at the moment and whiled away the time before going to bed.

Luckily enough – I love my wife and family and am blessed with a job I enjoy completely so I wasn't entirely devoid of purpose and joy in my life. I simply woke up and realized I was wasting a ton of time.

At the beginning of the 2019 – I made myself two promises. First was to spend more quality time with my wife and friends. We started travelling more as we went to Europe for 18 days, including time with family in Britain and our first European river cruise from Basel Switzerland to Amsterdam Netherlands. Next year – we're visiting Italy and Greece. It's a big World and we wanted to start seeing it together.

We also started to take dance lessons. It's a blast. We've connected with each other on a different level and made new friends as we are now part of a wider social network. The exercise has been good and again it's cut down on TV time.

The second thing I promised was to get this side hustle of mine up and running. I had two goals. First to create my own website, which I completed back in May 2019 and second was to write my first book. It's now the second last week of the year and by my rough calculations – I should be all done by New Year's Eve. It's a pretty empowering thing to actually deliver on one of your life goals. It's whetted my appetite for more.

None of this would have been possible without an idea and a life skill I could exploit. One of the great things my genetics and God blessed me with, is the ability to write. I'm certainly not an author of Pulitzer-Prize-winning quality – nor will I ever write something akin to Tom Clancy or Robert Ludlum. But, I *can* string together a page worthy of someone's time. I am further blessed to be able to write fairly quickly. It's a function of the fact I read – a ton - and have always tried to write as I speak which makes things flow fairly quickly.

Currently – I write for several magazines and have in the past written articles for one of Canada's largest daily newspapers. Given the fact I have this ability – and have the experiences to share with you as you've read them here – it made sense for me to write this book (and others I hope in the very near future) and run my own side business helping people like you. I welcome you to visit my website where you can learn more about my project at www.CatchUpInvesting.ca. Here you will learn more about what I am doing and why.

You can do the same thing.

While that may not be writing – it could be just about anything else. But you should make sure your side hustle is not merely a part time job (although there's nothing wrong with that) but is something that feeds your soul and drives your passion forward. You might have a hobby that can be monetized. Friends of ours have gotten in to hand-making signs, house decorations, art, weighted blankets and a whole host of other things they sell everything online and at crafts shows.

If you are looking for something more structured, you might start a unique home or online business or buy a low cost franchise. For me – I wanted to do something that wrapped up so many of the things that interest me and build that business over the next 5-10 years, at which time I may throttle back and enter semi-retirement. The key is to start now, keep your spending or investment in check and make this happen when you have the safety and security of a steady paycheque.

Be smart about it. Do this on your own time at the expense of your TV time – not your work time or else you might find your time frame somewhat… hastened.

Work Longer:

There is already a fair bit of mistrust and misunderstanding between the generations in today's work force. While Millennial workers soon will comprise the largest demographic in the work place – us Baby Boomers and older Gen X'ers still control most of today's senior positions. This is made more complicated as many Baby Boomers (according to Pew Research in the US) have little or no intention of actually taking full time retirement anytime soon.

There might be several reasons for this including the need to work to fund a more acceptable life-style and make up for a lack of savings; the need to work to help pay medical bills or debt and the genuine desire to work to help maintain a sense of purpose or enjoyment.

Baby Boomers are blamed for a great many things by today's younger generation and they have a right to be concerned. We Boomers have collectively failed to save enough, preferring to spend and borrow our way to better lifestyles. We have fostered a Ponzi-scheme-type social network of government support programs that will rely on fewer and fewer workers to maintain generous benefits and we have made a mess of the economy and the environment. Hint – a perpetually rising stock market is not necessarily a good thing, in and of itself.

And yet - while we have not been good shepherds, leaving all these living legacies – we are still the ones who need to bail out our kids and grandchildren.

Our need to help our Millennial and Generation Z off-spring as well as help care for our own ageing parents creates a unique stress all our own. Being caught between the generations is akin to being caught between the proverbial rock and a hard place. Our lack of saving – either from neglect, life happenstance or economic hardship is why so many Boomers will need to continue working, long after their conventional retirement dates. There is also no assurance social programs, like Social Security and the Canada Pension Plan are sustainable and that seems to create angst at every cohort along the generational divide.

If you are like me – you may continue working because you love what you do and find meaning and purpose in work. So may have said that if you love your job; you'll never "work" a day in your life. If that's true for you; then congratulations are in order. If not – then you need to stay current with skills training and the realization that you may not be able to keep working at your current level and pay. That may mean making compromises and cutting costs to the way you live your life.

Only you know if you can keep working at today's pace and whether or not you will still be marketable. The fact is you may not need much to help you bridge the gap as for many even a part time job will help pay for some of your monthly costs. If you want more from life and have the ability to travel and enjoy some of the finer things – then you need to take action today. I guess that's why we are here together, now.

By simply taking the steps to buy this book and read it – you are keeping up with the pace of coming change. But only by taking action will you actually get out in front of the curve.

Rental income from your present home:

The kids are gone! The kids are gone! Yay! – Now I can build that spa, home gym, home theatre, reptile sanctuary (huh?). Maybe you should give some thought to renovating the basement to include a legal income suite – or short term rental via Air BNB or VRBO – or perhaps open a Bed and Breakfast? You might even find a nice warm vacation home or cabin somewhere on the slopes and rent out your home, the months you're away? Hopefully there will be enough of a spread so you can fund the rental away from home and have enough left over to supplement your retirement living costs.

Just be careful and you do your homework to be sure you meet local regulations and address any gaps in your home insurance policy to be sure you're covered for whatever "mayhem" might ensue.

Hopefully by now your home will have been paid off and you'll have the flexibility to make active use of some of the space you no longer need. Make sure this is something that interests you as buying a rental property and living in the middle of one are entirely different things. Having renters live with you (be they long-term or short-term travellers and vacationers) will be a dramatic change of life for you.

There are certainly benefits from utilizing your now-empty space to add some extra cash each month. Only you can decide if that extra income is worth the change in lifestyle? What price do you put on privacy and a completely noise-free home?

Another consideration might be safety and security. Depending on the relationship you have with your tenant – they might be an extra means of safety and social support for you, as you age in place in the home you still love. Your tenant would be able to maintain the home should you be away on vacation and provide ready assistance should an emergency happen and help is required like emergency services (Fire, Police and EMT). This of course assumes you build a somewhat close and trusting relationship, which is by no means guaranteed.

Any costs associated with the renovation and ongoing operation of your income generator will certainly be tax-eligible expenses. Once again – consult the accountant and legal advisor-members on your personal board of directors to be sure before you commit to anything.

Let's consider the business case for starting a B&B.

Should you rent a room for $125 per night and are lucky enough to confirm 180 room nights per year; your income calculation might look like this:

Size of house = 2500 sq. feet

Size of B&B room = 180 sq. feet or 7% of total living space

Income generated = 125 x 180 = $22,500

Monthly Household Utilities and Insurance cost = (($1,800 x 7%) x 12) = $1,512

Cost of food = $24 per day = ($24 x 180) = 4,320

Net Revenue = ($22,500 – ($1,512 + $4,320)) = $16,668 or $1,389 per month pre-tax. The number would be higher if you operated for six consecutive months with your room rented every night. I will leave it up to you to adjust the math accordingly.

Now consider the fact your marginal income rate in retirement should be lower. Only you can answer the question; is this worthwhile? This extra income may in fact increase your reportable income and increase your marginal tax rate. Unless you are truly desperate for something to do and don't mind this additional tax consequence – then you might be better-off building that reptile sanctuary, or doing almost anything else. I may have missed a few items in my calculations – but this should give you a basic understanding of what might be possible.

The numbers would appear quite different and yet still compelling if you chose to rent out a basement apartment. Again – I'll leave the math up to you. I'm just making suggestions here.

Life Insurance:

As I am currently employed by a major Canadian Life Insurance company, I am precluded from speaking about Life Insurance to any great extent or in detail. I will only say that insurance contracts might offer you an additional means of saving tax deferred dollars while protecting your family. As such – I suggest you look for a qualified agent by asking your personal board of directors and friends for an introduction and discuss your options with your chosen advisor.

There are several strong strategies for individuals and small to medium sized business owners to utilize the structure of certain kinds of insurance products to help you along the way. Just make sure your goals are clearly defined before you confirm any contract.

Gold and Silver:

So many books and newsletters are available on the subject of investing in Gold, Silver and other precious metals and stones. It took us a while for us to get our heads around the notion that precious metals aren't actually assets. Shiny coins and bars do not produce cash flow and in some cases actually cost money to hold. There's no dividend and investing while in shares in mining companies may yield declared dividends, they aren't actually a pure play on holding the physical metal.

For our purposes (let's just say from here on) that whenever you see the word "Gold", that I'm referring to all the precious metals including Gold, Silver, Platinum, Palladium etc. That will save us both a lot of time.

Recall that we have so far referenced Chris Martensen's premise that primary wealth is created from the earth, usually in the form of resources and that holding, extracting and converting those resources to cash or some other currency is the only true form of wealth. Precious metals fit that description. While it is pretty much impossible for most of us to own a Gold mine – it is not impossible for us to own and hold physical Gold.

Gold can all be held as coins, bars and investor grade jewellery. We've all seen the ads on TV offering to "buy your Gold". Why are they so popular? Gold can be melted down and reformed into new items like new jewellery but also sold to be used in industrial processes and consumer electronics. Recovering these precious commodities makes recycling such an important concept.

The concept of mining a scarce resource has always appealed to humanity throughout the ages. Gold has always been a store of value. Gold has been linked to other commodities as a means of benchmark comparison. Economists and investors alike have compared everything from the price of an average home, automobile or the value of a stock index like the Dow Jones Industrial Average (Dow or DJIA) to the price of Gold. For example – historical values for the New York Stock Exchange have pegged the index at roughly 4 times the trading price of an ounce of Gold (specifically). If Gold is worth $1,000 then the value of the stock exchange should be roughly 4,000. As you no doubt have seen – today's valuations are WAY out of line with that historical valuation.

The range of trading values has been historically 1 times the price to 10 times the price of a single troy ounce of Gold in USD. Today's trading price for Gold is roughly $1,500 (as at Dec 28th, 2019 – opening value). The approximate Dow Jones Industrial Average on the same date was 28,650. That seems awfully high, relative to the price of an ounce of Gold in historical terms.

After having read several books by Mike Maloney, Jim Ricards and Dennis Gartman – I began to question that value of today's "cash money" to the value of hard goods like Gold and "houses" that tend to hold their value.

Stocks can fall to zero. There are a number of well-known examples. The value of Gold, land or an investment property is not as likely to see the same levels of catastrophic decline.

Consider also the fact that most trading currencies are no longer linked to Gold and now trade at floating values relative to each other in the Global marketplace. That means currency – or cash money (also referred to as "fiat" money) is valued on a country's economy, its tax base and the resources that fuel steady growth. Central banks in every nation control how much "money" is in circulation at any point in time – making more available, literally created out of thin air electronically or by physically printing more currency. The fact that in most cases, too much currency is created means the new cash cannot possibly be worth as much as the old.

Think about it for a minute. If something is more commonly available – is it worth more or less than it once was – or in comparison to something else that is scarce? That should be a pretty easy question to answer.

Think for a minute about all the uses there are in the World for each ounce of each type of precious metal and the fact that there is a real cost to mining and refining the stuff. Consider also that there are several examples of these minerals with dramatically declining stores in the Earth that are becoming more expensive and challenging to harvest. Such is the case with Silver today.

Silver is more often used in the creation of consumer and industrial goods than is Gold. World Silver stocks and proven resources are dwindling at a faster rate than Gold. If this is the case – then the relative value of Silver may increase in terms of price appreciation potential than almost any other precious metal.

Seeing that currency can be created from nothing by central banks and seeing that is not the case with precious metals – we decided some time ago to periodically start taking a little of our cash money and converting it to hold in Gold and Silver coins. For us – this was a decision to diversify our holdings one extra step. We decided that we needed some actual physical forms of the metals as stock prices could easily fall or be manipulated, that stocks did not provide true diversification and that Gold and Silver provided us with something of an insurance policy against everything else falling in value. Call it a currency conversion hedge and protecting our ability to maintain our standard of living, should the whole World economic system go into the toilet.

I'm not really a conspiracy theorist and I do not have a basement full of canned soup. I just think it makes sense if you're going to diversify, then it might make sense to hold something besides another mutual fund. No matter how much I like stocks, bonds and mutual funds; they're not the answer to everything.

My Cellphone costs me WHAT each month?

At the risk of sounding like I'm only advocating that you step over dollars to pick up dimes – that's exactly what I'd like you to consider.

If you're like us – you probably have a ton of monthly and annual costs that you blindly pay because they are set up to charge your credit card or bank account without a second thought. These costs have probably been charged and paid like that for years. Well, it's time to stop and be sure you're still spending money wisely.

Give some thought to the following:

- Do you still need a telephone land line? What are you paying for your cell phone and data? Can you get a better deal or cut back from a full service to a no-contract prepaid deal?

- Do you still need as robust a TV Cable or Satellite service – or would Netflix and other streaming services including Disney +, Apple TV and Amazon Prime work better in combination with a lower-cost TV package?

- Do you need all the streaming services I just mentioned in addition to Cable – or perhaps just one or two?

- What are you paying for insurance on home, auto, cottage, boat etc? Are all your policies with one insurer? Could they be? Should they be? You might be spending more than you need.

- Do you have 2 newspapers, 4 magazines and additional print and media expenses each month? Can you cut back? Have you heard about how many products and services are available at your local public library?

- What other streaming services do you support – Sirius Satellite Radio, YouTube and Spotify are all wonderful products and services that can be a suck-hole for your cash. Subscribe to too many at your peril.

The bottom line question to ask when you call the customer service line is – "Can I get a better deal?" You won't know until you ask and you might have to either threaten or even be prepared to move your business elsewhere. Customer loyalty representatives are usually empowered with better offers to retain customers.

Businesses often pay big bucks and absorb huge expenses to try and win new clients. The offers they make for the shiny new billing address do nothing for you so you need to remind these service providers that they need to keep you happy as well. As a long-term client – you are way more profitable to any of these companies simply because it will cost them a lot less to keep you engaged vs. finding a new client. The offers they make to you may be just attractive enough to keep you enrolled with savings you might not have thought possible. Like anything – "don't ask – don't get".

Saving $100 - $200 per month in incremental costs can add up to nice tidy sum at the end of the year. I suggest you think of making these "diving for dollars" reviews and phone calls at least once every two years and perhaps more frequently depending on the ads you see on TV and online. Don't be afraid to ask your friends and neighbours as well. You would be surprised at the cash we have saved in just the last 5 years by asking our new neighbours up on the lake where the best deals can be had.

Make and Keep a Budget:

One of the things diet coaches support is the idea of making and keeping a food diary. There is something quite powerful when you review a log of every calorie ingested over a set period of time (2-3 weeks or up to a month). The trends that become apparent reveal when you've eaten well, ate too much, not enough or simply included items that gave you nothing but a sugar high all too brief. The same could be said for your finances.

Make a commitment to yourself to track every penny you spend over a 30 day period. It likely won't be easy as you'll have to record the impulse-bought coffees and other discretionary items as well as the major costs like mortgage payments, car loans and utilities. You will need some sort of tracking device like an Excel spreadsheet, computer-based program like QuickBooks (online or software) or an old-fashioned paper notebook. Each tool will do the job provided you actually set them up properly and use them.

You will no doubt be surprised as we were when you realize the money you spend eating out, buying lattes, clothing, movie tickets or otherwise. Some of the very suggestions you've already read in this chapter will be revealed in a very material way when you start comparing what you pay with what you get and what you really need.

I am not necessarily suggesting you button-down everything so tight that you have no room for a few luxuries or wiggle-room to enjoy life. I'm just making the argument for exercising some restraint and setting limits to make sure you cover the basics and your need to save and invest while enjoying yourself at a more sustainable level.

The expression "living within your means" may be at face value somewhat "mean-spirited" but helps shine a light on the need to set some boundaries. These boundaries should be monitored monthly, evaluated annually and adjusted when increases or decreases in income are experienced. You just might find yourself in a unique position to expand your means rather than simply learn to live within the means you currently have.

The Bottom Line:

1. Small business owners and connected executives should investigate how they can release and capture wealth beyond what might be possible with RRSPs and the capital gains exemption. The question is – are you prepared to commit to a long term strategy between today and the date you expect to retire?

2. Could you free up an hour or two per day or week to start your own side business? If chosen well and managed properly – a side business would not only create income to augment your lifestyle today and provide an additional savings vehicle but give you a sense of purpose and focus in the years ahead.

3. You could continue working full time or part time hours to help stabilize your income and any shortfalls to keep you in the house you love or busy with outside activities that you might not afford in retirement.

4. The kids are gone. You no longer use your home gym. Come on – be honest – you never did. And you have time on your hands to either build a basement apartment or guest suite to rent on VRBO or Air BNB. Give some thought to whether or not you want to become an innkeeper and get busy.

5. Permanent Life Insurance (not term) not only pays a tax-free death benefit but provides the owner with certain tax-preferred investment options. There are many wealth creation strategies that can be made possible using features offered by insurance policies and readers should consult with a knowledgeable insurance specialist.

6. Gold and Silver have been called everything from "Real Money" to "God's Money" and perhaps for good reason. They come from the Earth and have throughout history been a true store of value vs. any paper money or fiat currency ever printed. Yes – they pay no dividends and may even cost your to store but in an uncertain environment and economy; would you be better-off with some real Gold and Silver in hand – or without? Your choice.

7. Set and keep a budget and control your costs. There is an old expression that suggests you can walk over dollars to pick up pennies and dimes. Let me suggest that you consider the dollars as your efforts to earn and keep

money while your pennies and dimes represent incremental savings; and they add up. Re-read these sections if you need to find ideas and inspiration.

CHAPTER 13

In Closing

The idea of writing this book occurred to me as a way to both "give back", recognizing what we learned and "pay forward", honoring the blessings we received. It also occurred to me that we couldn't possibly be the only people to have suffered financial setbacks and wonder if we had enough money saved to live retirement in reasonable comfort.

As I wrote the book, I kept coming up with additional ideas; "Oh I should include this idea or that product". As I sit here and type and edit these final pages, it is December 30th, 2019. It occurred to me a few days ago that I could include all manner of ideas and strategies. That put me in conflict in a number of ways.

First – my goal was to write about our personal experiences and I've already strayed from that by writing about a few real estate investment strategies we never used. I decided to break my original premise because while we have never flipped a house or employed BRRR – we have bought and rented

---

homes. While the process of BRRR is somewhat different than what we did – the main elements remain the same. We got into the real estate game, took a risk and have stayed the course. I think we can safely claim a position of integrity on that matter.

Second – in all honesty, I can keep coming up with ideas and additional examples of the investing strategies and continue writing this stuff for many more months. Two things will happen. Life will get in the way and I will never finish this damn thing. That would be a complete failure without upside as this book represents something of a promise I made to me; one I need to keep. I've always wanted to write a book and after a couple of false starts, looked at this time and effort as being different. This time – I had a story to tell and it was ours.

My goal was to share our experiences and the fact we did indeed learn some tough lessons along the way. Having to do it all over again – I would have decided to look for opportunities in Ontario as well as in Alberta. I would have avoided Northeastern BC altogether. We did all the right homework - and still - made a decision that wasn't quite as good as the ones we made elsewhere. I guess that's proof positive that the best laid plans are still prone to the "shit" that happens.

I think we will be alright long term in BC. My gut tells me that we will have overpaid for an "OK" asset. In the end – we will still have benefited from a professionally managed property with clients (tenants) who will pay the lion's share of the mortgage each month and hence make our money work more efficiently. It is just that we will have done better elsewhere over the same time frame.

The current soft market in the Alberta oil patch does give us some level of concern but we were wise to choose investing near Edmonton instead of in or near Calgary which seems harder hit in this oil market collapse. The Edmonton market (we hold in a little town called Spruce Grove) tends to whether these storms much better as it is the provincial capital and nothing says stability like government jobs.

In total however, we were not wise in skipping options closer to home in Ontario.

In choosing Alberta, our thinking was to avoid the rent control, tenant-centred policies governing the relationship between landlord and tenant. Perhaps that was a mistake, given we elected to use professional property managers who would have protected us from some of that hassle.

We now find ourselves in a quandary where we'd like to hold additional properties but are reluctant to become over-leveraged. The natural solution is to seek joint venture partners who would be willing to invest the down payment and jointly qualify for the mortgage.

Investors who are open to this idea would be protected by having all the freely available "after-all-costs-paid" cash-flow paid to them until their down payment is paid off and then join in the net profits and cash-flow of any deal equally. This would be a departure for us from the path we've taken to date and represents something of a learning curve for us in structuring the legal framework of such partnerships but, we do have the resources and coaches available to us to keep both all parties safe and a number of interesting investment strategies to consider.

We have done well and continue to be confident in each of the private equity (PE) positions we hold and will likely seek more. To date, they have just made sense and have provided good returns. We've been lucky as so often these PE investments have failed or taken a long time to materialize for others in the past.

We know there are even more attractive investment options but that these come with significantly higher minimum qualifying commitments. I read somewhere that the smart money – the old money – invests where others fear to tread or where they are never invited. At some point we may go there when we unwind (IF we unwind) our current real estate holdings.

I do believe however that we will likely continue to hold our individual properties and leave it up to the kids to keep them or sell them to pay off the taxes owed when we're gone. While I am still working, it makes sense to pay income taxes owed today on the rent we receive and lessen the tax burden on them, tomorrow (hoping of course I am using the term "tomorrow" figuratively).

We may discuss changing our rental income tax management tactics with our accountant once I've elected to step away from the day-to-day gig where I am currently happily employed. We'll see what options we may have at that point and resist rushing. My wife tolerates the fact that I want to work another 10 years, which will take me to Age 69. Since my dad worked until he was 72 (he too loved what he did every day) then I consider myself lucky and perhaps somewhat lazy.

Now What:

Writing the book has by and large been the easy part of the Catch Up Investing journey. Now we venture into the unknown.

The manuscript needs to be formatted and edited and an attractive book cover for every version needs to be designed. I plan on editing my own writing – even though I'm reminded that a lawyer who represents themselves in court more often than not has a fool for a client. What can I say? Fortune favors the brave and sometimes hopefully, the foolish?

Apparently the big thing now is to have our work properly formatted so it can be read on any Kindle device and printed on demand for those who want a traditional reading experience, turning pages and making notes in the margin.

Then the book needs to be uploaded into some sort of Amazon Kindle Direct Publishing account, I have yet to build and finally, the book needs to be promoted, hopefully differentiating it from every other non-fiction, self-help investor manual. I am sure the list of available Kindle reader options and competition will be HUGE! So again – thank you for selecting, purchasing and reading my book!

Fortunately – my wife Susan has volunteered for the marketing job and as she has been fully retired for the past 5 years has the time available; after all – "every day is Saturday!" (Her words, not mine). We'll see just how much she still enjoys the job in 6 months or else I may be looking to take on more work myself or finding a qualified "propeller-head" here in Canada or from some far-off land. Up-Work has been a true savior!

I have no humungous expectations from having written "Catch Up Investing". I only wanted to document our journey and share some of the insights we learned and we hope you've found this to be of value.

Are you looking for Help?

By now, you may have visited my website, www.CatchUpInvesting.ca. There you would have read some of the information I've covered here but none of the background and stories, which I hope have helped move you forward. I am here to help and am happy to answer your questions and connect you to the people I keep on my own personal board of directors. Nothing would please me more than to help you take your first steps on your own Catch Up Investing journey.

Even though I may be of help to you, I suggest you always do your own homework and seek expert advice from other sources. After all – what I have to share may not be right for you. I can only share that the majority of our decisions and moves have been right for us.

You are more than free to use the ideas we shared and find your own path.

What I learned when I was on Bay Street, working with hundreds of Canadians at their dining room tables and in their kitchens and living rooms is this; it is far better to be "approximately right" more often times than it is to be "precisely wrong". Even though growth happens at the margins and when you push the limits of your existing comfort zone – you've got to be able to sleep at night.

Some or all of the strategies we've shared with you (so far) may also be "approximately right" for you. All of them may be "precisely wrong". None of them come with guaranties and again (I must sound like a broken record by now) you need to do your homework and read everything before you sign anything.

With that, Susan and I thank you for having purchased our book. We trust our having documented the past 10 or so years of our Catch Up Investing story provided you with some new ideas. Use them as a starting point to chart your own path. We wish you all the very best of luck and good fortune!